ADVANCE PRAISE FOR *TECH BOSS LADY*

"Adriana shares her valuable learnings about the world of Silicon Valley startups with the next generation of founders. This book is a how-to guide for leaping into the world of tech entrepreneurship, with tips on how to navigate leadership, partnerships, fundraising, innovation, stress, failure, and more."

—Jonathan Abrams, Managing Partner of
Founders Den and Founder of Friendster

"In *Tech Boss Lady*, Adriana brings her authentic and powerful voice together with those of other women trying to make an impact in the technology sector. The lessons learned and bon mots of advice will be greatly appreciated by any woman—or girl—navigating careers in start-ups and technology companies."

—Fran Maier, Founder & CEO BabyQuip

"This is the story of us—the makers and hackers and dreamers who built Silicon Valley. It's a survival manual for the girls who lead, who challenge authority, who are made to feel "less than" even while they are changing the world. . . . I so love that Adriana wrote this, I so love her story, and I so love her voice. And, just like back in 2007 when we *needed* Adriana to start Girls in Tech, we also *needed* her to write this book. Because as women who lead, who invent, and who strive, we will only get by with a little help from our girlfriends."

—Wendy M. Pfeiffer, CIO Nutanix

"A practical guide to the fast-paced start up world from Silicon Valley to New York to 150 chapters across the globe! Adriana, has lived the lows and highs of entrepreneurship and shares the little known but important things she learned. For example, taking the plunge and pursuing your start up full time and not trying to moonlight for too long—leads to lack of focus and possible burnout. This has been a fast-paced journey and is reflected in every page of this book. Every aspiring entrepreneur, girl or boy, should read this book!"

—Anu Shula, Serial Entrepreneur,
Rubric, MyBuys, Tapjoy, RewardsPay, Botco.ai

"If you are starting or thinking of starting a company you MUST read this book. Gascoigne gives an honest, firsthand view of managing stress, raising money, and coping with failure. Along with wisdom from twenty-two women leaders in tech, you'll be well prepared to conquer the world!"

—Charlene Li, *New York Times* Bestselling Author
and Founder of Altimeter, a Prophet company

"Adriana Gascoigne's very personal stories in her book *Tech Boss Lady* inspire the reader to be the authentic 'you' as an entrepreneur and leader in a very dominated male tech world. I could not put the book down as I often saw myself in these stories. Thank you Adriana for writing a book that inspires both women and men to be better!"

—Monique J. Morrow, President The VETRI Foundation
and President, Co Founder, The Humanized Internet

"Somehow Gascoigne manages to deliver a broad range of insights into how to launch and run a business as well as bringing out your inner bad ass, all in such a down-to-earth, powerful, and highly entertaining way. Deeply inspirational and practical."

—Danielle Feinberg, Pixar Animation Studios

"There have been countless times when I have looked around a room and realized that I was the only person who looked like me. *Tech Boss Lady* is a practical guide for anyone who has ever been in the same situation and felt intimidated or unsure of what to do next. The honest guidance is not only actionable but refreshing—I only wish I'd had a book like this when I started my career."

—Rathi Murthy, Chief Technology Officer, Gap Inc.

TECH
BOSS
LADY

TECH BOSS LADY

HOW to START-UP, DISRUPT, and THRIVE as A FEMALE FOUNDER

ADRIANA GASCOIGNE

SEAL PRESS

Seal Press
Hachette Book Group
1290 Avenue of the Americas, New York, NY 10104
www.sealpress.com
@sealpress

Printed in the United States of America
First Edition: June 2019

Published by Seal Press, an imprint of Perseus Books, LLC, a subsidiary of Hachette
Book Group, Inc. The Seal Press name and logo is a trademark of the Hachette Book
Group.

The publisher is not responsible for websites (or their content) that are not owned by
the publisher.

Print book interior design by Jeff Williams

Library of Congress Cataloging-in-Publication Data

Names: Gascoigne, Adriana, author.

Title: Tech boss lady : how to start-up, disrupt, and thrive as a female founder /
Adriana Gascoigne.

Description: First Edition. | New York : Seal Press, [2019] | Includes bibliographical
references and index.

Identifiers: LCCN 2018051369| ISBN 9781580058285 (hardcover) | ISBN
9781580058308 (ebook)

Subjects: LCSH: Businesswomen. | Women-owned business enterprises. | New business
enterprises. | Leadership in women.

Classification: LCC HD6072.5 .G37 2019 | DDC 658.1/1082--dc23

LC record available at https://lccn.loc.gov/2018051369

ISBNs: 978-1-58005-828-5 (hardcover), 978-1-58005-830-8 (ebook)

LSC-C

10 9 8 7 6 5 4 3 2 1

For Mom and Dad. For teaching me the ropes.

CONTENTS

How to Use This Book   *xi*
Introduction   *xv*

Part I ✳ On Being a Tech Boss Lady

1. What It Takes   3
2. Being a Woman in Tech   19
3. Intrapreneurship   29
4. Business for Good   43

Part II ✳ On Start-up Essentials

5. On Stress   55
6. Partners   67
7. Advisors   81
8. Building Your Team (Thoughts on Hiring)   99
9. Innovation   117
10. Confidence   131
11. The Pitch   147
12. Leadership   165
13. Failure   175

Part III ✳ On Girls in Tech

14. What I Know Now   189
15. What's Next   197

HOW TO USE THIS BOOK

THIS START-UP BOOK won't be like the others.

I know what you're thinking: *"Real innovative, Adriana! Another start-up book!"* Or maybe it's something like, *"Aren't you supposed to be from Silicon Valley? Aren't you supposed to do new things there?"* Or maybe it's just: *"I'm confused. You say you're Mexican, but you look Japanese. Which is it?"*

This book is written for first-time founders around the world. First-time founders of any business. Tech founders. She bosses, they bosses, and he bosses. It's for those of you who can't stand reporting to someone else because you know deep down inside that you *should be* that someone else. It's written for anyone who has ever dared to dream of the possibilities that lie just outside the margins of convention, the ones who itch to solve a problem and won't stop until they've at least tried. It's written for all of you whose hearts beat to define your own fates.

This book is written for founders of all kinds, but don't get tripped up about the "tech" aspect. Frankly, you're kidding yourself if you don't consider yourself a tech founder. I don't care if you're in the business of fashion, pet-sitting, cosmetics, health care, lemonade stands, time machines, whatever. We're all tech boss people. Every business today relies on technology to scale.

It's also written for those of you who work in the start-up world as a non-founder and those of you who take charge in the corporate world. Start-up founding team members. Intrapreneurs. Tech workers. Just because you're not at the helm of the ship doesn't mean you don't affect its course. The advice shared in these pages belongs to you, too.

This book is meant to show the real side of start-ups; the gritty underbelly of start-ups that so many people don't understand until they experience it themselves as first-time founders. I want to discuss topics that make even the most veteran of founders uncomfortable, like failure, insecurity, and disappointment. I want to tell you what happens behind the shiny logos and before the launch events. I want you to understand the realities of what it takes to build something from scratch, forged from willpower, iron determination, and just enough ego to see it through—because it's going to be harder than you believe, I promise.

But I can't just use my story—that would be a disservice. I want you to also hear it from female leaders who have been there before us and survived—and the ones who are in the thick of it this very moment. That's why I met with more than twenty badass female leaders in tech so I can deliver their war stories and sisterly advice straight to you. Learn from their challenges and experiences. Apply their advice to your own goals. My hope is that you close the book with a better understanding of what you're about to get into.

Start-ups have a sexy appeal, but I want to show you what they look like in the squint of early morning light. Like what you might see after an amazing night out on the town and a one-night stand: no six-pack, off-brand briefs, back hair that would make a bear jealous. The stealth-farts infiltrating your silky bedsheets and the halitosis may make it hard to remember what was ever appealing about your choice in the first place.

Now, this isn't to downplay the sexy side. Oh, the sexy side! I imagine it like the bright lights of a Broadway show. In fact, I often feel that way even today. Being your own boss, even being an "intrapreneur," is the gateway drug of entrepreneurship. You're holding the reins of your destiny, and the doors to any limitations—real or imagined—have been knocked down. It's you and wide-open range, baby. Do What You Please Land. There, decisions flow freely, red tape doesn't exist, and the stakes are high.

There's an inherent adrenaline rush in the idea of being your own boss and breaking away from the safety harness a regular office job provides. Beyond giving corporate America a solid kick in the groin, you have the satisfaction that every minute you give to your venture is for *you*. Your dreams, your vision, your product, your name.

Yet. Few start-ups will become the next TechCrunch darling.

Here's what you know, or think you know: You're probably going to fail. You may never get funded.

I know this. Of course you do.

You've probably also considered the huge punch in the face your personal finances are going to take. Pasta and cheap beer every night, and cut the manis and pedis, you hear me?

Yeah, I've thought about that. Of course you have.

You've probably thought about the massive amounts of cash you're going to need to make your dream happen. Taking checks from friends, family, strangers. The promise that's made when you accept that money.

No shit, Adriana.

Well, it's not enough. What you think you know—it's not enough. It's only going to take you so far before you get sucked into the start-up undertow. I want to warn you. To prepare you. I want to open your eyes so you understand what you're walking into.

I wrote this book to tell you what it's like to walk in a beat-up pair of start-up shoes. I wrote this book to put you inside the minds and hearts of founders, advisors, and experts across Silicon Valley, to share their stories and insights with you. This isn't about flowery stories of inspiration (though maybe you'll find some hope here). This isn't about making you feel good (no one will care about your feelings). This isn't a book of success stories or winning (though many people we've spoke with have found, or are on their way to, success).

It's the story of what it really takes to pull it off. It's the low points and high points of many people's journeys. It's the insights and anecdotes from Silicon Valley insiders on what they've experienced and what they believe is needed to survive start-up life.

And it's the story of Girls in Tech. My story.

I want this book to get as dirty as real start-up life. I want you to rip out pages. I want you to scrawl in the margins. I want this book to get trashed at the bottom of your hipster San Francisco messenger bag. I want this book to bear the stains of your greasy late-night taco truck run. I want you to use this book as your personal stress ball, token of hope, and punching bag.

Because this shit is hard.

INTRODUCTION

LET'S KICK THIS party off with a flashback. Year: 1989. Location: Westlake Village, California, an idyllic community of three- and four-bedroom homes, vibrant green golf courses, and public schools good enough to make even the biggest private school snob give a begrudging nod of respect.

I'm twelve and experiencing puberty in all its glory. My features are playing a game of Ms. Potato Head with me; nothing seems to fit my face. I'm rocking a fuchsia tank top, a slap-bracelet, and roller-skates—the real deal, with laces. I'm at my mom's travel agency in Oxnard, just north of where we live. It's the weekend, when I can push myself around the foyer without worry of slamming into customers. Paula Abdul's electric voice blasts from the radio. In a few minutes, my mom will hand me a stack of flyers, warm from the printer. It will be my job to skate through the grocery store parking lot and hit each car with a flyer advertising her travel agency services.

This was my first experience with entrepreneurship.

❋

I didn't grow up knowing *exactly* what I wanted to do. But I knew the kind of life I wanted. My parents set the example for me: my dad was a technical writer for Walt Disney's

Imagineering arm, crafting meticulous manuals on how to put together and fix each and every ride. Growing up, my dad was always around the house. I never wondered where he was, because he was always home. He asked about my day. I helped clean his office, and I filed his work papers. But it wasn't all paper stacks and filing cabinets; in the afternoons we'd squeeze in one of our signature daddy-daughter burping contests. (My future boyfriends would learn that I belch better than a hippo.) These days were my earliest lessons in the concept of work-life integration; the idea that I didn't have to separate the two has stuck with me ever since.

My mom immigrated to the United States from Mexico. She was one of twelve kids. She had few other choices in life but to hustle. After working for Mexicana Airlines for years, she discovered a far more lucrative career that still had all the perks of the travel industry.

So, she opened her own travel agency and rocked it. In fact, at one time she was doing so well that she made more money than my dad. It was a family business. My sister and I worked there on the weekends and sometimes after school. I was often tasked with creating my mom's flyers and keeping the front desk organized.

I didn't see my friends as much as I wanted to. But, as a family, we all understood that we worked together, and we took care of each other. Just like kids have faith in many things—their parents, teachers, Santa Claus, rainbows, the spooks under their bed—I grew up believing that if I worked hard, it would translate into the life I wanted. I didn't receive a paycheck per se, but my allowance money was all I needed to grab a movie on the weekend with friends or to save it up for DVDs and CDs (remember those?).

I didn't connect the dots between entrepreneurship and my roller-skating flyer girl persona until much later in life. I knew I didn't want to be—*couldn't be*—stuck in a corporate job. It wasn't that I didn't want to work hard; it was that I couldn't stand the idea of being put in a box. Corporate jobs come with corporate job descriptions. There's a chain of command, rules, a thick employee manual. Pay grades and volumes of HR stipulations that say you can only get *this* percentage raise a year, or that you can only make *this* much with *this* title. Even at a young age, these concepts felt claustrophobic to me. I couldn't stand the idea that I could be hired to do one thing and limited in my ability to explore and do another.

Start-ups offer just the opposite experience, especially at a very early stage: there's so much to do and so few to do it. Those who volunteer to take on extra responsibilities are heroes in this situation! Rules hardly exist. There's probably no HR. Projects are up for grabs, and small teams can be nimble. Few people will tell you no if you want to test an idea or dive into a new project that isn't in your original job description. All hands are wanted, ideas welcome, and duties negotiable. This made sense to me. It sounded far more appealing than being boxed into a stuffy pay grade or job title. At start-ups, I knew I could be just as free spirited and fast flying as my roller-skater persona wanted to be, tearing down the halls and getting things done.

It was settled. The corporate world wasn't for me.

☀

Some know early in their careers that they want to come to San Francisco and immerse themselves in its start-up ecosystem—arguably the best in the world. Me? I zigzagged my way here. After graduating from UC Davis with a degree in sociology and a concentration in organizational studies, I hung around LA for a year, working in marketing and advertising. I landed in San Francisco for a quick year to work for Chase Communications before returning to Los Angeles for an opportunity in consumer brand marketing strategy. Later, I moved to Miami to work for a real estate development company for nearly three years. And then a job for a worldwide PR agency brought me full circle back to San Francisco. But it was the next job, heading up marketing for an online video start-up in 2006, that made me stay. It took a few attempts to "stick" to San Francisco, but, once it happened, there was no way in hell you could rip me away.

I still feel this way today.

Now, about that start-up. It was an online video start-up—not the porno kind, the Netflix kind. It was truly cutting-edge, before its time. I had been poached from my ad agency to come lead the product marketing strategy. I breezed through the interview process, and I was ecstatic to get the gig. I had a big title. Good money. Real-world responsibility. I felt like a badass.

Here's the deal. All the rumors you hear about start-ups and the stereotypes you hold—well, they're true. I can verify it myself, as I walked into the cliché on my first day. Ping-pong table? Check. Shiny flat-screens with March Madness news bites scrolling nonstop? Check. A bunch of dudes making fart jokes? Check. (Okay, I may have gathered around the ole water cooler for that one.) But you get the idea. It was like walking into a man cave masked as an office. And I was the only woman, aside from a receptionist, at a company of thirty dudes.

There was no build up to it, no peaceful first few weeks. The harassment kicked off as soon as I received my company-issued Mac. The inappropriate e-mails poured in that fast.

You smell good. Gross.

I love what you're wearing. Your ass looks great in that. This one made me want to crawl into a potato sack and call it a day.

What are you doing tonight? Uh, buying a Costco-size batch of pepper spray?

I even had a water bottle thrown at my head when I was on the phone with a reporter. (No, I'm not making this up. If I was, I'd think of something a lot more creative than water bottle abuse.) And it wasn't that I couldn't catch the damn thing; the mountain spring water came along with a refreshing side of, *"Shut the fuck up!"*

Rather than squash the issue from the get-go, management's brilliant solution? Offer me a corner office on the other side of the building. Sure, I loved the kick-ass view of downtown. But it was a flashy prison and a shameful excuse for a solution to a pervasive company problem. I was isolated from my team, unable to collaborate. I might as well have been working remotely.

I realized I was working with a bunch of kids running wild on a playground. Welcome to the start-up world, Adriana.

※

Two things came from my experience there. One: despite the harassment bullshit, I still loved start-ups; I loved technology. It was the first time I was really in my element in a start-up post-PR job, post–real estate. A bunch of assholes couldn't deter the sheer joy I experienced from building something. Playing a key part in the early stages of a company felt right. It's profound to see a product come together and to know it's from you and your team's hard work and sweat. When you work around the clock and you get your hands dirty under the hood of a start-up, you earn a right to be proud. *Look, Ma! I made that!* Two: despite this incredible satisfaction, I realized I couldn't be the only woman in tech who experienced a similarly unfriendly, sexist work environment. I saw that I was isolated, but I instinctively knew there were others like me, sprinkled at start-ups across the city, feeling just as alone. Apparently, a lot of women poop while giving birth. Whelp. My shitty experience led to the birth of Girls in Tech.

You know the saying, "find your tribe"? My initial mission was just that: find other women in tech. I had survived for a year and change at the video start-up. But, by this time, I was depleted. I was pissed. I was downright *sad*. I was supposed to be doing what I loved and working on projects that made me feel alive. But, instead, I woke up every day with a pit of anxiety in my stomach. This is a physical reaction to the anxiety that comes from being bullied and harassed at work, the place you spend most of your week. It was a year in, and I didn't feel safe there. My body said so.

It was as though the veil had been lifted on something that I thought I loved and trusted. The tech industry was exciting, fast paced, and innovative—all the things that pulled me in like a magnet. But it was also rampant with sexual harassment and hostile toward women. If I was going to march on, I owed it to myself to build a support system.

So, I looked for one. But there wasn't anything out there for women who were early to mid-career who just needed a support framework. Who needed to see that they weren't the only ones going to work in a man cave every day, they weren't the only ones passed up for that promotion, they weren't the only ones receiving creepy new-hire welcome e-mails.

So, I did what every entrepreneur does when she stumbles upon a problem with no solution. I set out to create a solution myself. I spoke with friends about it. I went to sleep at night, thinking in hazy abstracts about what it could all become. Months passed until one Saturday, when I visited my fashion designer friend, Jeff, in his sunny studio apartment.

We snacked on sushi and stared out his floor-to-ceiling windows at the San Francisco skyline. In the corner of his apartment sat his drafting table. Strewn across it were colored pencils, paper, scrap paper with notes on them, samples of soft leather, his laptop. The tools of a modern artist. Seeing his sketches— the stick figures of women, the splashes of color, the messy and loving nature of his work process—inspired an instinctive urge to share my own aspirations.

"I have an idea," I started.

"Well?" he raised said, eyebrows raised. *Do tell.*

"I want a way for women in tech to find each other. There's more of us, out there. But we need to find each other. I was thinking of creating a group or putting on some events."

"You've got to do it."

Such confidence! For him, it was such a no-brainer. But that's the way Jeff operates. Have an idea? Just get 'er done.

"I was thinking of calling it Girls in Tech," I said. "It's not for girls, it's for women. I mean, I suppose it could be for girls. But I want it to be *fun*. I don't want it to feel stuffy. I want it to be hip. I want people to be excited about it."

He turned to his laptop and clicked on whatever design software he used at the time. In a matter of minutes, he whipped up a logo. The "Girls" he made cursive; feminine. The "Tech" was blocky and digital. And then he paused, briefly, before adding one last detail: a pair of eyeglasses hanging off the *T*.

That's when things became real. That logo didn't just represent an idea; it represented an organization. That logo carried Girls in Tech through its first few years. Having that logo in a file on my laptop meant something. It gave my idea shape; it made it feel official. In those moments, my idea went from being whimsical to having weight.

Eyeglasses on the *T* and all.

⁂

I must address the Girls in Tech name here, now, because I can't let this book pass me by without taking an opportunity to do so. I get put over hot coals on the regular for the name of my organization. A lot of people have a problem with it being "girls" in tech rather than "women."

When I started the organization back in 2007, I was hyperfocused on the fact that there didn't seem to be any "cool" organizations for women in tech. I didn't want to create something that rang of a lecture hall; I didn't want to give the group a name that felt robotic or sterile or . . . well . . . not fun. Perhaps this was the marketer in me putting her foot down. To attract members and grow, I wanted women to know that we were relaxed, that you could come to our events and meet other "girlfriends," and that it was going to be anything but stuffy. I think it's fair to say the brand has held this standard since day one, when women came to our launch event in San Francisco and entered a club via a playground-style slide, for God's sake.

We've grown up a bit (bye-bye, slides), and our events certainly raise the standard for grittiness and rawness. That's the way we like it. That's what I envisioned more than ten years ago, and I think that's what women need and want. A no-apologies forum. Our speakers get up onstage and feel comfortable dropping an occasional F-bomb. Our events connect women—but not in a transactional manner; they're connected because they find real joy in meeting other badass women in tech. The realness, the casualness about our programs has lent itself to a real community feel, one that I don't think the word "women" would support to the degree that I'd like. Nope. I don't want to be perceived as buttoned up. I don't want to dull down our color and vibrancy. I don't want to extinguish the youthful impression that our name evokes. That's a light I only want to allow to shine brighter.

But. Women get angry that we don't call it "women." To some degree, I see where they're coming from. Would men flock to an organization called Boys in Tech? Unlikely. But men also don't refer to their buddies as their boyfriends. They say they're going to go hang with "the guys." I could go on, but I'll leave it there.

Girls in Tech is *all inclusive*. We do have a handful of teenagers show up at our events, and we love that too. We also have men (dudes, boys, guys, whatever). My goal isn't to diminish our maturity or our credibility or to lose supporters. I suspect that our members get it and appreciate the playful nature of our brand. We like to think that we speak with the energy and spirit of a girl, that all of us women members share a sort of girlish connection and fierceness.

＊

So, armed with little else than my hastily made logo and gumption, my vague notion of "women connecting with each other" became Girls in Tech. It was 2007. It was springtime in San Francisco, and the fog was clearing, and the city air hung with optimism.

Ultimately, Girls in Tech launched with a single event: a networking night at a dance club downtown. I'll admit, I didn't go into the evening with a lot of goals, or even a lot of strategy. All I knew was there had to be other women in tech out there and they probably felt alone, like me. My goal: get us all into one room and have us step out from the shadows.

There was just one problem: I didn't have the money to pull it off on my own. So, in typical Silicon Valley style, I pulled strings to make it happen. My friend Jonathan Abrams, founder of Friendster, was co-owner of a night club downtown called Slide. The club was appropriately named. One literally had to go down a giant slide to enter the place, like a twenty-one-and-over Chuck E. Cheese's. The space was donated to our cause for free and from nine 'til midnight, Girls in Tech owned the dance floor. It was a deal I couldn't pass up.

My marketing strategy? I used Facebook to get the word out, and I urged friends to share. I called every chick I knew and asked her to tell every chick she knew. Then I waited. It was me, my logo, and our first (humble) offering to the women of the San Francisco tech community. If you had asked me the night before how it was going to go, I would have told you I was wondering the same thing.

The day of the event, I was in heels in a city Target, struggling to push my shopping cart full of wine. With the bottles clinking and my heels tapping, I made my way through the store to check out. I don't remember what wine I bought (*lots*). I don't remember what cheese and crackers I bought from the grocery store after. But I recall a distinct feeling of optimism.

Flash forward to Slide, 9 P.M., I'm too busy cutting cheese (literally) to be nervous. I'm cutting cheese like I was born to do it and frantically opening bottles of wine. That was the deal: *the space is free and you're on your own for drinks, Adi*. I didn't want the women to have to worry about drinks; I just wanted them to show up. In the dimly lit background, a DJ spun the top hits of 2007, and, one by one, women slid into the club (how often can you say that?) to see what Girls in Tech was all about. It was only later that I learned that a long line of men formed around the block around this same time, just waiting for their chance to join us at midnight when our "freebie" time was up.

Here's what happened while they waited outside. More than two hundred women showed up in their start-up uniforms of jeans and whatever else they felt like wearing that day. There was zero agenda to the evening other than giving women the experience of looking around the room and seeing that they were not alone. I'm sure I said a few words. Frankly, I was overwhelmed. It was a powerful evening, witnessing women coming together from all roles in tech and realizing that, yes, there is power in numbers. That night, something within me ignited. I had caught the attention of these women. It was time to make something real happen.

The potential at my fingertips was mind blowing. It still is today. In those early years, Girls in Tech focused on networking events and panel discussions. I leveraged connections at Stanford and Berkeley, and I called any VC I knew. We hosted presentations on fundraising and financial modeling and branding. Women collaborated and pulled each other up. Girls in Tech quickly launched in Los Angeles, then New York City, and soon after in Kuwait of all places! Turns out, women around the world are interested in technology. And they're drained from fighting mobs of men to make it happen.

＊

Nearly ten years later, Girls in Tech Kuwait is still thriving, with the same managing director who originally kicked it off. As for me, I now manage a team of eighteen employees and consultants. If it seems tiny to you, it's huge to me, especially after being the solopreneur for so long. *My baby is walking!* Additionally, we partner with a talented team of freelancers and contractors. We keep things lean and scrappy. I primarily work in Girls in Tech's San Francisco offices, but I also work wherever I happen to be in the world. Leading an international nonprofit takes me to all corners of the globe. I've logged into my laptop from Melbourne, Taipei, London, Barcelona, Paris, and back again.

My days are filled with weekly sprints (hang tight, and I'll explain more when we talk about intrapreneurship), partner meetings, coffee catch-ups, and event logistics. Most meetings happen onsite, but it's not unusual for me to zoom all over the city and the valley, heading to meetings and taking calls by car. Yes, we've grown tremendously, but you wouldn't necessarily know it if you spotted me at my little coworking desk in the open floorplan.

I spend most of my time doing virtual handshakes. I tell the Girls in Tech story to anyone who will listen. We focus heavily on co-branded programs with corporations (we wouldn't survive without them) and on annual events. Events are a huge piece of Girls in Tech, even ten years later. Getting together and supporting one another in person doesn't get old.

We are women in tech. We are teens in tech. We're male allies in tech. We're Girls in Tech.

As Girls in Tech spawned new chapters around the world, we've evolved to create our own trademarked programs. Today, we have more than 100,000 members at sixty locations around the globe. Our members are CIOs at some of Silicon Valley's tech darlings; they're mentors; they're mentees at all stages of their careers. They're college grads; they're young women interested in learning how to code; they're entrepreneurs finding their way.

They're this amazing global force, a powerhouse of women helping other women. Girls in Tech's global army of badass women is an embodiment of all the *good* that occurs when women stick together. This is what progress looks like. It's the silver lining of our collective story as women in tech, of all our frustrations, of all our setbacks, of all our joys, of all our steps forward. We may be scattered around the world and we may not speak the same language, but we have a common interest in helping each other, backing each other, lifting each other up, and working to create real change.

This is Girls in Tech, ten years later. Not too bad, huh?

(If you could see me, I'm beaming.)

PART I

On Being a Tech Boss Lady

CHAPTER 1

What It Takes

I'M NO EXPERT in the human psyche, but there's one trait I see in every entrepreneur I meet: absolutely no fear. Entrepreneurs are stupidly unafraid. They're unafraid of failure (or so they say, more on that later); they're unafraid of the next steps, of the unknowns. No plan? No problem. No money? Who cares. No expertise? They'll find the way; they'll discover answers as they go.

It's as though we entrepreneurs were built without a safety setting. We were built without an off button. We're bursting to be sent on a mission. We're a bunch of fireworks just dying to be ignited—*someone, please, light that damn match!*—we're water waiting to roar into a boil. Or that inconspicuous car on the road, begging for the thrill of a race.

But what does it *really* take to foray into entrepreneurship? What do entrepreneurs possess in the microbes of their guts that sets them apart from others?

When I think about what it takes, I think about my mom in the humble early days of her travel agency business, of the way she blindly rolled up her sleeves to aid others, her quick-witted, resourceful nature. She's still this way. And my dad, who started his own business when I was about ten. It was his defiant rebuttal to corporate America and his determination to lead a life of flexibility for his family (long before the days of flex hours and all that warm and fuzzy HR stuff). And I think about my mom's mother. For most of her existence, my grandmother in Mexico was extremely poor—the I-don't-know-how-we'll-eat-today kind of poor. She had to dig deep to feed her family, yet she dug even deeper to help others, and without a moment of hesitation. And I think of my grandfather, who came to Mexico from Japan, without any knowledge of the language, no idea what he would do for money, unsure of the path before him.

It's magnetic, the way my thoughts constantly return to them. These four serve as eternal compasses on my entrepreneurial map. These were people who didn't think about the consequences, only what they needed to do in the very moment they were in. They thought about the next steps rather than letting fear of the unknown take hold. Perhaps that's what drove them and fueled them to first survive and, later, thrive.

My grandmother grew up in Mexico, in the small colonial village of Guanajuato. She met and married my grandfather—we called him Papa Carlos—when he came to Mexico after being turned away at the border by US authorities. He was on a mission with a friend, in search of adventure, new opportunities, a new way of life. But after being so quickly dismissed by the United States, he couldn't face his family in Japan before he had even found a sense of footing abroad. So, he did what any entrepreneur would do: he pivoted. He turned south. Mexico 1, US 0.

In Mexico, Papa Carlos worked in, and owned, a garden variety of businesses: he worked hard labor on a pig farm—yes, it was everything you imagine it might be, from the filth and the mud to the blood and the squeals. He worked in a local watch shop, where he learned the mechanics of fixing watches.

For a while, he owned a restaurant. He took up anything and everything he needed to keep a roof over his family. But my favorite was his candy factory—how many of us can say their grandpa had a freakin' candy factory like Willy Wonka? As a kid, I thought this was nothing short of incredible. He specialized in hard candy, like taffy, caramel, and lollipops. But, more importantly, he made jobs for hundreds of families throughout his town. He's an example of the real current of economic progress that so many forget: entrepreneurs. (You and me, reader. We're the real job creators.)

By the way, just because Papa Carlos owned his own candy factory, it doesn't exactly mean he was rich. Most of the kids in the family took turns working in the sweltering heat of the factory to keep the business churning. My mom has a scar on her leg from where boiling hot, thick caramel spilled over on her when she was just a teenager. It seeped into her pants and clung to its cotton threads. When workers peeled back the layers of her pants, her skin went with it, revealing a raw, bloodied wound that today reminds her of the sacrifices her parents made to stay off the streets. That scar was a symbol to me throughout my childhood, of family togetherness, hard work, and commitment. (I suppose hard work and the idea that it will always lead to good isn't just in me because my parents worked hard to create a better life here in the States. It has its roots in Mexico, where grit saved my family and helped to catapult our success here today.)

And my grandmother, you might as well call her Mother Teresa. Okay, an exaggeration, but not uncalled for in my eyes. She once helped a woman give birth among throngs of people in a crowded, dusty street in her town. I couldn't dream this up. It's true.

She took people in on the regular: orphans, travelers, people who were down on their luck, friends and strangers who needed shelter for the night. Her business was her family. Granny had twelve kids. Managing a household with that many children was a business in itself, especially without luxury conveniences like nannies, UrbanSitter, and maids. The children had just one pair of underwear each, and one shirt and one pair of pants. These were worn daily and washed nightly. (How's that for co-jones?) They ate the simple food of Mexico—beans, corn tortillas, and rice. They were happy to have each other. From that perspective, they lived grand lives.

While you're already aware of my roller-skating escapades in support of my mom's travel business, my dad was just as influential to me. When I was about ten, Dad quit his corporate gig and went out on his own. He created technical manuals for any kind of product that needed one. Printers, airplanes, manufacturing, assembly lines, rides, and games. Beyond the benefits and allure of being his own boss, it also served as an F-you to corporate America. By this time in our lives, he had experienced a layoff or two; the scariest happened right after we moved into a new home in Los Angeles. I'm guessing I was about five years old, but I still can feel the sadness that shrouded our lives at that time. It should have been a bright highlight in our playbook—a beautiful new home in an affluent area!—but, instead, life was shadowed by uncertainty, piling bills, and disappointment.

And so, Dad made his own path, where he didn't have to worry about any uncertainty other than whether he could deliver to his clients. While my mom crawled through the grisly Los Angeles traffic—three hours, round trip—to make it to her job at LAX / Mexicana Airlines, Dad worked from home and held down the fort. He led school drop-offs, packed lunches, showed up when I was sick. He was the one who helped with homework, arranged playdates, and did the kid-shuttling across town to take us to ballet and art class.

In fact, this started long before he was his own boss. In my youngest years when we lived in San Pedro, and regular daycare or babysitters weren't an option because money was tight, I was often dropped at the local YMCA. I vividly remember him packing my lunch and me pleading with him to let me stay home.

"It's just for a while, Tuner," Dad said. "Just for today, love." (I have no idea why he called me Tuner, but I like to think it was about something cute related to a cartoon rather than a tuna fish.)

"Dad." My voice came out in a strained whisper. "Please, don't send me to the Y."

"Just for a while, Tuner."

"I'll be good if you let me stay. Let me stay. Please, Dad."

He would pack my lunchbox—I think it was My Little Pony—the old-school metal sort, and drop me off. No doubt, I eventually came around and played with the other kids, but what I remember most is just sitting on the steps in my dress, waiting for his return. Dad still tears up when he recalls these times. It was a season in our lives when my parents were dead set on creating a better life for us. And that meant we all made sacrifices, even me. My toddler-sized sacrifice was a day at the Y.

These four—my grandparents and parents—steered me on the path to entrepreneurship and the nonprofit world. They lived their lives doing good: in business, in the street, among strangers, at home with friends. They led with their hearts, and I played witness to their passion. I knew that such a life, one of entrepreneurship, of following your dreams, of taking charge, was possible. I knew because it played out before me, every day of my childhood.

✳

So, I'm not going to say that anyone is or isn't made for entrepreneurship. My goal isn't to discourage you or to say who is or isn't fit for the lifestyle. That's not my business. But there is a theme I've seen across entrepreneurs. Every entrepreneur I know—and I mean *every single one*—isn't afraid. It's a startlingly consistent trait, I'm sure many in my circle would agree. There must be something to it.

My advice to you: if you are afraid, ask yourself why. Listen to your fear. And think about whether you're ready to push that fear aside and get moving. Pay attention to your inner voice, to your habits, to the way you tackle or avoid problems in your life. If you consider yourself an entrepreneur, do you have the resilience that it will take? There's a lot to be said about moving to your own beat, but think hard about whether you're actually meant to join the band if you're already feeling so out of place.

The lack of fear is quickly followed by acute urgency to propel forward. You want what you want. *Now*. You have a vision, a spark, an idea, and you'll crawl out of your skin until it's realized. Your entrepreneurial dreams invade your life, a demanding army that takes over every conversation, your shower ruminations, your daydreaming, and your bank account. The urgency is surely obnoxious to those on the outside, probably because no one understands or cares—with every breath—as much as you.

The people who don't make it in entrepreneurship, they have zero urgency.

Business columnist Harvey Mackay wrote about urgency: "Ask any entrepreneur to list the keys to getting a company off the ground, and urgency will be among the traits listed. No matter how intelligent or able you may be, if you don't have a sense of urgency, you'd better start developing it now. The world is full of competent people who honestly intend to do things tomorrow; however, tomorrow seldom comes for them. Many individuals with less talent are more successful because they understand the importance of urgency. In other words, get started now."[1]

The problem here is that many first timers just don't move, period. And that's when it's over before the ride has even begun. Some people languish in the comforts of thought and preparation and strategy and number crunching and analysis.

The planning process becomes like a velvety security blanket. These folks roll out the welcome mat for a solid case of analysis paralysis. They cling to a plan and, *holy shit*, it must be the perfect plan. Their planning and the analysis create a safety harness for complacency. There's a deep satisfaction in figuring out every little detail before moving forward.

Does this sound like you? If you find yourself in this rut and you're paralyzed by analysis, there are two routes. The first is to ask yourself *why?* Why are you so afraid, and what's holding you back? What is the worst thing that could happen? The most confident founders—even the ones who fail, and we know that nearly everyone will—are not afraid. So, you need to ask yourself what makes you hesitate and do some internal digging. Play therapist.

But here's where I get harsh: if you're talking yourself out of your idea or feeling so inadequate, maybe now is not the time to take it on. It's only going to get harder. This is only the beginning of an uphill climb. If you don't have the calloused hands, bulging muscles, and thick skin to start nosing forward, then maybe you should hit the bench and sit this one out. The earliest start-up stages aren't environments where second-guessers thrive. I talk about the need for confidence in Part II. Confidence (even if you're faking it, and, trust me, I've been there) folds into this idea of moving forward fearlessly. Start-ups innovate in real time, and there's very little room to map out every move, to calculate this and that, to act in slow motion. The beginning should be a time of curiosity and excitement to solve a problem. If you can't get that far, that is, if your excitement can't override any fears you're feeling, then that's not a good signal for your start-up prognosis.

Now, if you're just a procrastinator . . . well, welcome. You have plenty of friends here. That's an entirely separate issue, one that plagues most of humankind. This is a matter of focus and prioritization. My advice to you is to know how you work, and work with your strengths and weaknesses. This may mean using a project-management system, getting serious about lists, or even partnering with a cofounder who can keep you organized. And I know it's been said by many smart people before, but make goals that you can achieve. For me, it helps to schedule my time, hour by hour, and plan what tasks I'll be working on. This forces me to not fixate on knocking out a whole project at once, but rather on achieving baby steps on the daily. I go into every day feeling empowered rather than overwhelmed.

As far as an overall plan, let me tell you a dirty secret: *I'm not a details person.* Sometimes (usually?) I throw spaghetti at the wall and see what sticks. It's messy—disgraceful, really. I skip ahead to marketing plans before a program is polished. I hold meetings without agendas. I plan events and let the details fall together in this beautiful haphazard way. For me, it just works.

I'm not bragging. Hell, a lot of people would be embarrassed to admit this. But here's my take: things move fast, and whatever you think you're doing on day one, it's going to change much more than you will ever know. Some of the changes can be soul crushing—that is, if you're not open to them. You may wind up with a completely different product. And if you're doing things right, you'll be okay with that because you're continually transforming your business into something that people need and want. That takes change and courage.

Some people obsess over the details. I throw spaghetti. I'll talk about this more later, but, for now, let's get back to what it takes.

OTHERS WEIGH IN ON WHAT IT TAKES

Heidi Roizen is a legendary venture capitalist who started numerous businesses and advises many start-ups; plus, she teaches entrepreneurship at Stanford University. She considers two attributes critical for entrepreneurship: a growth mind-set and tenacity.

Heidi referenced Carol Dweck as an expert in the growth mind-set concept. She's a renowned Stanford psychologist and author of *Mindset: The New Psychology of Success*. Dweck has dedicated her career to studying how people achieve their goals—and what sets those people apart from those who flounder. A growth mind-set is all about navigating the obstacles in your life, figuring out what you can do (versus fixating on what you can't), seeking opportunities to improve rather than resigning yourself to being stuck in a situation or place in life. Essentially, you're taking control of how you feel about your life circumstances and failure, rather than simply throwing in the towel if things get tough.

Of this concept, Roizen said, "You have to be constantly learning, adjusting, seeking and understanding data. The startup business is a very messy business and you have to understand how to adapt."

The second thing Roizen says an entrepreneur must have is tenacity. "[This and growth mind-set] go hand in hand. To me, tenacity is, even when the data is bad, you figure out how to get up and keep going. . . . If you get kicked down and stay down, you're going to stay down forever. You have to keep getting up and starting over again, every time you hit an impediment, every time you have a failure. . . .To me that idea of tenacity and that willingness to learn from your mistakes and get back into the game tomorrow is what differentiates the entrepreneurs who ultimately win and those who don't."

Personally, I would add focus to Heidi's list of what it takes. The first start-up I worked at, ever, was like YouTube before its time. We sure had the tenacity and we had the growth mind-set, but, as things grew more complex and heated, we lost all sense of focus. I was there for about a year and a half. The early days were filled with late-night scrum sessions, strategy meet-ings, fast prototypes, and down-and-dirty marketing strategy. There was a sense throughout the company that we were on the trajectory to creating something valuable. From a team and warm-and-fuzzy perspective, it was everything I envisioned start-up magic to be.

But, eventually, the company pivoted to focus on soft porn. The CEO sort of disappeared and went on an adventure of his own, seemingly losing interest in the core business. The CTO then attempted to be a CEO but was far more suited for a technical role. The entire leadership team was dismantled, and we lost a vision for what we were working toward. It was as if we were hamsters, running on a wheel to nowhere. The magic fizzled out.

In a start-up environment, you can't lose sight of focus and productivity. Life is so busy. Everyone is all about multitasking and juggling competing priorities. We're all just trying to do too much, too fast, and it can create a pile of tasks disguised as progress.

Mercedes De Luca is former COO of Basecamp. She's an experienced C-level exec, having raised VC and led an early-stage start-up. Her take on productivity and focus: "It's not about work-life balance. It's about doing what matters." She takes something so many of us struggle with and puts it into the simplest of terms. (These words belong on a poster in every coworking space.)

Mercedes's personal hack for productivity: every morning she draws a T-bar on a piece of paper. It's the divide between the must-get-dones and the nice-to-get-dones. Anything in the must column not only must be worked on that day, but it also needs to contribute to the big-picture goals. And she tries to knock out the important stuff first thing in the morning, when she's fresh.

"The problem with most companies is they don't have a clear focus on what matters. They have people working on and doing things that don't matter. Time wasters. . . . You don't need [to work] 70 hours if you're doing what really needs to get done. But it's hard for most people to not try to do multiple things at once."

Mercedes alluded to parenting as a great example of how we can try to do too much. Every parent wants to give their kid exposure to many different activities. You want Timmy in karate, in swim, in Spanish and piano. You do this because you want to help him find a passion. But, with this approach, your child can never focus on just one thing. What if you were to allow him one thing?

"The people who become Olympic skaters or swimmers focus on one thing," Mercedes pointed out. "A lot of founders are like ADD—lack of focus can end up killing the company."

Here's another take on the guts of entrepreneurship. Venture capitalist Mark Suster has often written about the DNA of an entrepreneur. He lists eleven traits that make up an entrepreneur (attention to detail is one of the traits he lists; Mark, we'll have to disagree just a tad there—you can hire people for that!). One of his pieces focuses on the willingness to accept risk, or—as he put it so well—have cojones. While my grandmother had cojones to deal with her twelve children's undies every night, Mark is talking about the leap of faith that is required for a successful venture into entrepreneurship. This leap might include quitting your job, putting in money and relying on that credit card, asking friends and family for money—or other sacrifices that only apply to you.

"If you put on paper what it would take to be successful in your company, you'd never take the first step, which is why most people don't," Suster writes. "It is often called a 'leap of faith' because you jump from safety into the abyss with only the blind faith that you'll find a way."[2]

Did my journey to entrepreneurship look like Suster's template? I'd be lying if I said it did. My moment of takeoff felt more like getting electrocuted than a poetic lightning bolt of inspiration. I had been running Girls in Tech on the side for a long time—almost eight years—and I relied on a team of volunteers and a few close partners to execute. I didn't quit my job, not for many years. Instead, I hummed along at a slew of start-ups and nurtured the organization in the moonlight.

This isn't to say I didn't believe in Girls in Tech or that I wasn't committed to the vision of the organization. I was. But because the organization is nonprofit and because it relies on volunteers, it didn't have the same cutthroat vibe that you may associate with many of today's start-ups. The organization supports women in tech, but it hasn't historically created tech itself. (That is, until now. Our career recruitment platform, exclusively for women, launched in 2018.) Girls in Tech connects women all over the globe, but we're scrappy in the sense that we have a low-budget, small team.

Readers, don't be like me. Don't wait so long to take the leap. I should have done it sooner, but I waited until I was on the hook for serious money to make the move.

One day, I received an e-mail. I was in my office at RxMatch, a health-care start-up, when my phone lit up. It was a notice from the event coordinator at the Kimpton Hotel in Phoenix.

Subject: Invoice for your conference

Dear Ms. Gascoigne:

Please review the attached invoice for your spring conference. Your first payment of $33,000 is due on March 1, 2015. Please review, and let me know if you have questions. We look forward to hosting you.

Kind regards,
Maya [I'll call her Maya]
Marketing Coordinator [I'll call her a marketing coordinator]

Okay, not so bad, right? No, the heart attack occurred when I opened the attachment, which was an invoice for a nearly six-figure bill. $95,000, to be exact. I don't recall the specifics of my reaction, but it was in the category of *What the Fuck?! Holy Shit. Fuck! I'm FUCKED!*

Even when I think back to it, I still feel that way. It hits me like the sting of an old scar, and it still burns, even now, years later.

That invoice was for $95,000 that I didn't have. Not even close. Nor was it even remotely in the ballpark of what I expected to earn from the Catalyst Conference, which is now Girls in Tech's largest annual event. At the time I received this Mother of All Bills, Catalyst was exactly sixty-five days away. We were selling tickets. We were booking speakers. We were still figuring out lights; we didn't know what we were serving for lunch. I may have had just one sponsor lined up. And I was on the hook for $95,000 when I expected it to be less than half of that.

My Girls in Tech partner—the closest thing I had at the time to a full-time employee—had signed the deal, and it was done. I didn't know this was coming, this wasn't in my plan, believe me—I actually knew that she was reviewing and signing an agreement (as she was the person on all calls, contract negotiations, etc.), but the BIG difference is that I understood that she (and a team that she put together) was committed to leading and producing the conference. Instead, she left. I had a full-time job, so I wasn't planning to be involved in the conference production. I was fucked, and no amount of sweet talking or bullshit or negotiation could uncoil the contract. (Believe me, I tried.) After my mind—and jaw—slowed from the endless F-bomb slur train, I came to life.

Here's what happened in the next twenty-four hours. I resigned from my job. I had a six-figure bill, but fundraising duties called instead—and that meant being available for meetings with corporate executives. Moonlighting doesn't cut it for that sort of thing. No VP wants to meet you at 9 P.M.; you need to be available in the daytime. I went straight to work, dialing every person I knew who was somebody and anyone I knew who knew somebody who could help. I called friends to ask whether they had connections at big tech companies. I called former colleagues and bosses. I called my parents and cousins. I was bold and brash and asked for what I needed in a way I had never done before. I stayed up all night putting together a presentation about Girls in Tech—who we were and what we were out to achieve. It was time to do the thing I wasn't comfortable doing, hadn't been comfortable doing, what I'm still uncomfortable doing: I had to ask for money. It was time to sell.

It was time to own my role as an entrepreneur. I had spent the past several years teasing the idea, half committed, pretending. But that ugly invoice changed everything. I no longer had the luxury of just dipping my toes in the waters.

It was time to dive in, fearlessly, sharks and all. I had a start-up to save.

WHAT DID WE LEARN?

✓ **You can't be afraid.**
Fear sets us back on a lot of things in life, but there is no greater setback then failing to pursue your dreams. If you're afraid, ask yourself why. Ask yourself, What is the worst that can happen? Challenge your own beliefs about your start-up idea and your capabilities. I still think about where Girls in Tech could be today if I hadn't taken so long to make it a full-time job. Dive in or get off the shore.

✓ **You must have a sense of urgency.**

If it's not important to you, it won't be important to anyone else. You have to act like every project is critical, because it is in the beginning. Big ideas are wonderful, but if you can't execute, you have nothing.

✓ **You must embrace a growth mind-set.**

No one should be more optimistic than the founder. You'll feel as stuck as you allow yourself to feel. Get comfortable with being in sticky situations, and treat them like mazes rather than brick walls.

✓ **You must remain focused.**

You can work your ass off and roll up your sleeves and think big—but these will only get you so far if you don't know what you're working toward. Entrepreneurships require focus. Keep running and keep working hard, but know the direction you're headed—or else things will crumble beneath your feet.

CHAPTER 2

Being a Woman in Tech

OF COURSE, I did end up saving Girls in Tech, but you know that. Our existence today is a spoiler. Before I continue my story and talk about the essentials that come with every start-up experience in Part II, let's talk about the reality for women in tech today.

As I write this, women across the country, across all industries, are calling out by name the male predators who have incessantly harassed them. They're telling their stories. They're pushing back their veils of shame, emerging from the shadows. Their pain has hit a boiling point. These men have exploited women behind a shield of power, money, and fame. They've used their resources and their stature and their ability to influence their companies and industries to evoke fear, to make women feel as though they have no other choice.

The sheer arrogance of it all. The egos. The notion these men hold, that they'll never get caught. The masks they wear of do-gooders, of family men, of community leaders—it's all fake. And it makes me furious.

What happens at the likes of Uber and Zenefits—the parties, the sex, the brogrammers, the frat-boy atmosphere, the blatant disregard for any sense of a normal and professional working environment—doesn't happen everywhere, but it is way too common. This is what happens when you get a lot of men pouring out of school with technical degrees and ideas—and they get money from other white guys who are a decade or two older, with a lot of money and ideas, too. One generation funds the next, and on it goes. Brogrammers spawn more brogrammers.

And when it comes time to hire, guess what? Men hire who they know. They hire people they have relationships with already. They hire people their buddies recommend and trust. By the way, who doesn't do this? Women certainly do. This is something we all do, and we can't knock men for it, but there's a cycle in progress. It's tough for women to hop on the merry-go-round once it's in motion.

I know a lot of people—men and women—in positions of power who tell me all the time, "I want to hire more women. But where are they?" There is an undeniable talent pipeline challenge. I *know* there is a pipeline challenge. Women are fighting for jobs at the leadership level, but there just aren't enough women with the skills to truly compete for the open positions. Tech roles are and will always be in high demand. Everyone is looking for reliable engineers, talented UX folks, rock-star product managers. Ladies—where are you? *Come out, come out wherever you are.*

A few changes will help to fix this issue, developments that are already underway. One, we need more women in leadership positions. Women founders who are in control, funded, looking to hire a whip-smart team (ahem, women!). Women at the top can pull in other women and help to lift them up.

We also need men to lift women up. We need men at the top to step up and take on a new challenge. If they don't know talent that fits their bill, I challenge them—why don't you? Why haven't you stepped beyond your comfort zone and expanded your network? Come to any Girls in Tech event in San Francisco, and you'll find yourself surrounded by a sea of passionate women, talented women, savvy women. Women who have the potential to lead your teams, scale your start-up, transform your product. They just need the key to get in the door.

To these men, I want to say, look for women. Make it your mission. Ask around. Come to events. Post your job in places you wouldn't otherwise post it. Let your network know that you're in the business of supporting people from all backgrounds at your organization. And don't discount your internal talent. It's critical that you build your own internal talent pipeline and send that elevator back down. You may look around your organization and dismiss the people you have available to you. But give those beneath you the respect of having the conversation first. You might be surprised by what you learn about your team's experience or who comes forward to express passion about moving into tech once you lay out the welcome mat.

And yes, we need to rebuild the population of women who are eligible to take on these positions. Some people don't want to hear this, but there's an obvious population difference. It needs to be fixed. Somewhere in the '80s, women started dropping out of STEM programs. Somewhere along the line, they were told they did not belong there. They came to a lecture hall and found themselves the only female. They were doubted; they were pulled aside and told they may feel more comfortable in art classes; they were assumed to need extra help studying for that course; they were whistled at. They were spoken down to; they weren't called upon; they had their thighs grabbed underneath the tables; they didn't have support at home; their parents persuaded them to study humanities instead; they were told they were too pretty. These women were overlooked, dismissed. They were told they should focus on meeting a man and getting married; they were told they'd make a great teacher or a wonderful cook. They opened their high school and university textbooks to pages filled with men in lab coats. They had men come to guest lecture the class. Their future became blurred, and over time they struggled to see themselves in it. They lost sight of what they wanted and who they thought they were.

I know this. Because I've spoken to enough women—women who persevered through this—to know. These stories are real. These things happened, and they still happen.

As for the women who persevered, as for the women who made it, as for the women who have climbed to vice president or C-level roles? Well. They still get overlooked. They get asked to take notes in board meetings. In interviews, his eyes might travel down to her chest. They don't get asked for their opinion. They get called honey and sweetheart—too many times for it to be a forgivable slip. Hands slip around their backs, lingering just a moment too long. They get talked over in meetings. Their ideas get lost, unrecognized. They don't get credit. They get paid less. They get passed over for promotions more often. They get cornered at the office Christmas party. Their commitment is questioned. If they fight for their team or their idea or their budget—whatever—it must be "that time of the month" or they're just in a bitchy mood that day.

And female founders—that's a whole other bucket o' fun. Women get less venture capital than their male counterparts, as in they only received 2 percent of VC dollars in 2017. *Two. Percent.* This was pulled from a recent *Fortune* article.[1] No, I didn't leave off a zero, and, yes, you did read that right. The saddest part is that it increased in 2017 from the prior year, by a smidgen.

As the same article frames it, "While the #MeToo movement may be altering some aspects of the VC landscape, it hasn't yet translated into many more dollars for female founders. All-women teams received just $1.9 billion of the $85 billion total invested by venture capitalists last year, according to data [from the] M&A, private equity, and VC database PitchBook. That's equal to about 2.2% of 2017's total pot. Meanwhile, all-male teams received about $66.9 billion—roughly 79%."

WOMEN, BABIES, AND START-UPS

Talia Goldstein is founder and CEO of Three Day Rule, a curated matchmaking start-up based in Los Angeles. People had to apply to join the website, and only certain people would be accepted. In addition to the dating site, they also offered offline matchmaking, face to face, and then they had matchmaking events. Eventually, Talia and her team shut down the online matchmaking portion in a dramatic pivot: they chose to focus entirely on getting matchmaking right. Today, they target people who are willing to pay thousands of bucks for an extremely catered and curated experience. Love life, outsourced.

Now, imagine going through the ups and downs of start-up life as a woman but also raising venture capital while pregnant, as in taking VC meetings at nine months. Yowza. That takes guts. I say this, by the way, not to be against it—I'm a woman too for God's sake—but because her actions go so much against the grain of what's accepted in Silicon Valley. Heck, her being a female raising capital goes against the norm. Add pregnancy to that bonfire, and I have no doubt that she scared the bejesus out of the men investors she met with!

Talia was pregnant for two fundraising rounds, actually, her small seed raise and her VC. For her seed round, no one knew her happy little secret. She was so early on, she could hide it. She was also encouraged to hide her pregnancy based on the feedback she stealthily received from some advisors. Before she raised her seed money, she had read a blog article written by a very prolific Los Angeles investor. In the article, he explicitly stated that he would never invest in a pregnant CEO. Never. This article led her to call all her advisors—without telling them she was pregnant. She casually mentioned seeing the blog post and asked them what they thought, and whether they would ever invest in a pregnant CEO.

They all said no. Each one.

"I felt like I had no other option but to hide my pregnancy. It was a very strange time. I should have been excited to be pregnant, but I felt very ashamed. I hid my pregnancy. I didn't even tell my business partner. Then I started to show, I told my partner and we stopped fundraising," Talia said.

Fast forward, and Three Day Rule needed to raise bigger bucks. Talia was pregnant again.

"I thought, I'm not doing this again. I'm not hiding this pregnancy. I've grown this company. We have the metrics. People should invest. I thought—for all women out there, I am going to prove that we can do this. I wore tight dresses. I was super pregnant and enormous. I just owned it. I didn't apologize. We ended up raising $1.2 million in this round."

But here's the catch: of the nine investors in Three Day Rule, no one actually met Talia in person to see her pregnant. "Every investor knew me before or gave me money after. There was something about seeing me pregnant, no one would give me money."

Talia worked right up until her due date. She was asked to spin around on video calls to show male VCs her pregnant belly. They commented on how huge she was. They wanted to see it. They delayed further discussions about her deal. *"Let's see how things go with the baby."*

"It was just an interesting experiment," Talia reflected. "The people who I spoke with on the phone, who had no idea I was pregnant, invested. It never came up, there was no reason to tell them."

This story isn't meant to discourage you. Ladies, I'm telling you this to *prepare* you. This is real, and this is what it's like to be a woman trying to raise money pregnant. If this is you, or you think it's going to be you, think now about your strategy. Prepare for massive disappointment, but also consider how you'll handle it in general, whether you'll say screw it and wear the tight dresses and refuse to apologize for something so many women endure and choose. Prepare to shock the crap out of male investors who don't understand what it's like to overlap a career and motherhood. These guys have never had to choose.

There's no reason why you can't be a mom and raise money and lead your start-up. There will be trade-offs. But don't expect everyone to understand that. You have to overcome deeply embedded societal expectations.

But Talia got through it, and that's something. That's hope.

MONEY WILL ONLY GET US SO FAR

The recent #MeToo movement sheds light on something that most women in tech know: Being a woman in this industry, run mostly by white dudes, it's complex AF. It's not something that companies can just throw money at. The Facebooks and Googles of the world can't just hire an experienced human resources leader, confer the title "head of diversity" or "vice president of diversity and inclusion," send out a press release, and pat themselves on the back. The problem doesn't end there, though I wish it were that easy. (Don't get me wrong, I appreciate these efforts. I applaud these efforts. My point is that things can't be simplified to that degree.)

Additionally, I'm a believer in starting early to get women exposed to STEM. As early as in eighteen months to two years old (talk about pipeline and long lead times!). I'm not talking about pressuring a toddler to study the planets or telling a kiddo to major in mathematics. But I am talking about maybe gifting your niece some badass dinosaurs for Christmas versus yet another sparkly tutu. How about giving her some Legos or airplanes from the "boy side" of the toy store? What about asking your kid's preschool to launch a rocket, to build a model erupting volcano, to start telling little girls that they are smart rather than pretty? (Remember, this is coming from *moi*, a self-diagnosed dress addict.)

Women of future generations, I want you to know: you can rock a pair of heels, wear a dress with attitude, and still go to the moon.

NOT TO BE A DOWNER, BUT . . .

Here's the crappy reality. Being harassed, catcalled, and made uncomfortable appears to be woven into the fabric of women's lives. It doesn't just happen to one woman, it happens to *all women*. It's a common thread, connecting each of us. I wish I could tell you a single woman who it hasn't happened to.

I can't.

It happens in and out of the office. The catcalls in the street. The possessive glances in a bar. The whistles from cars going by, the guys who step just a little too close.

I want to tell each of these men that he may be a father one day, to a darling little girl. And I want to ask him to step back and think about how he can pave the way for the world to be a better place for his daughter. I want him to imagine the opportunities that may or may not be available to her. To, for once, let his heart get upended at the idea that his brilliant ray of sunshine may get harassed too, may be told no. May be overlooked, discredited, minimized. Soul crushed.

And then I want to ask him what he's going to do about it. What changes can he make today to make her tomorrow safer?

And yet there's a silver lining still. Please, don't take my frustration and deep disappointment in the issue as a signal that all is lost. Something *is* changing. In fact, I haven't felt this much hope, ever.

Even just a few years ago, you wouldn't have seen these headlines about sexual harassment. You wouldn't see the diversity panels or hear about women being in high demand for board seats. Just the act of talking about it is a strong starting point. It makes people uncomfortable to discuss it, men in particular, but it's the beginning of massive change.

The lack of diversity in tech and the rampant sexual harassment are becoming issues that are socially acceptable to call out. They're being recognized by media, by leaders, by the masses as a problem. To that I say yes! We can't pretend it's not there. This is the beginning of change, and it's a beautiful thing to watch. History is happening before our eyes. I have never before seen this level of action.

So, yes. I feel more hopeful than ever.

We can also play a part in nudging that boulder forward. We ladies, we need to get better about owning our achievements and being as brash and bold as men. We need to ask for more and believe that what we're asking is worth it, whether it's that promotion, a salary increase, or VC dollars.

We need to virtually link arms and support one another, without fear of being pushed aside or missing out. We need to see a landscape before us, one of opportunity enough for every woman, not just the few who elbow their way in.

We need to call out our harassers. Shame them, publicly. We're seeing the power of this now. Women are speaking up, and, yes, men are afraid. It's safe to assume that there's a hell of a lot of men out there mulling over the way they've treated women, regretfully, and they are afraid. As they should be. With this continuing dialogue, there's going to be fewer and fewer places for these predators to hide.

Now that's something to celebrate.

WHAT DID WE LEARN?

✓ **There's never been a better time to be a woman in tech.**
I mean it. Despite all of my grumblings, I do feel this way. Women who are coming into the tech and start-up community today have more resources at their fingertips than they did five years ago, and certainly a decade or more ago. There's a community out there waiting to support you. There are more companies, mentors, and VCs than ever willing to listen. The dialogue is all around you. People recognize it's an issue, and the good ones want to lend a hand. Take it.

✓ **Own it.**
Ask for help when you need it. Negotiate for the salary or capital you think you deserve—and then more. Become more optimistic and bold with your start-up projections. Go on, get a bit cocky. In other words, act a bit like a man. No one is going to give you a hand out here, no one cares about how you feel, and no one is going to bend over to help you unless you make that call. So make it.

✓ **Link arms with other women.**
Women talk a lot about supporting other women, but—guess what—we can still be catty as hell. Make it a goal to support other women. Start this week. It could be an e-mail, a phone call, an introduction. Do your small part in helping other women achieve success, because one woman's success is a collective win for all of us. Don't trick yourself into thinking that there's not enough to go around for everyone. The more women we can lift up, the more women we can pull up. Let's work together to create our own cycle.

CHAPTER 3

Intrapreneurship

AS I SAID earlier, this book isn't just for founders, it's for all of us. I'm an all-inclusive machine. I want to champion the rock-star leaders who operate within organizations every day to push them forward and drive them toward innovation. This one is for the intrapreneurs of the world: part entrepreneur, part corporate ninja. I hope you're listening.

Just a few weeks ago, I was working late in our San Francisco offices. Outside, dusk was falling, and the skyline was coming aglow. Inside our shared office spaces at RocketSpace, a co-working space where we gratefully set up shop each day, I was tying up some e-mails and gathering some papers to head home to Oakland for the night.

Tamar, Girls in Tech's director of marketing, approached me with an idea. She told me she had woken up the night before with a spark of inspiration for our International Women's Day campaign; it struck her in her sleep like lightning, and she'd been up since 4 A.M. drafting concepts. The big day was approaching—a major holiday for an organization like ours—and it occurred to her that women need to "brag" more, that women tend to be too humble about our accomplishments. Not enough of us readily claim our achievements and tell others proudly. Rather, we tend to meekly get our work done and move on to the next task, hoping to get noticed along the way. (And we see how well that works, right?)

"So, I was thinking, *brags*. Women need to brag more," she said. "How about Lady Brags?" Tamar explained the concept: women take turns "bragging" online about their accomplishments or nominate other women in their lives to do the same. The idea was to have it go viral across social media beginning on International Women's Day.

I stopped pushing papers into my messenger bag; Tamar had put me on pause. "How are you thinking that we execute it?" I asked.

And of course, T. had it mapped out. She was ahead of me. *As usual.*

"I've already put in a request for some content and I circled over to the team to get their feedback," she explained. "I also pulled together some graphic concepts that I think will work and . . . "

She went on. She had it figured out. She was putting on a display, right in front of me, for every reason why I hired her. She spoke confidently, excited; this was a woman with a vision. See, Tamar is Girls in Tech's resident intrapreneur.

Welcome, intrapreneurs. You're a new kind of entrepreneur on the rise, the type of entrepreneur who is only just being recognized in recent years: the intrapreneur, or entrepreneurs within an organization. I know you're not founders of a company per se, but you're founders of *ideas*, of initiatives, of risk-taking action. You exist within start-ups, within global enterprises, and everywhere in between.

And you are often the real superheroes behind any great company's success.

Does this sound like you? Intrapreneurs are the people who will take an idea and run with it, little to no direction required. They rally the right folks together to get something done. They say yes to taking on more. They naturally gravitate toward projects outside of their on-paper job description. They have a workhorse-style attitude about getting shit done. They're ridiculously motivated, have admirable self-initiative, and create on their own.

If you're nodding your head yes, congratulations. You're teeter-tottering between the world of stability and start-up high. Which side will win?

Here's my own little intrapreneur tale. When I was working at Ogilvy & Mather in between start-up gigs, Intel was my top client. Talk about a mammoth organization! Sprawling, extremely corporate, and structured. I was in charge of developing the digital strategy for the Intel Insider program. The campaign took something as high tech as the Intel computer chip and made it a commonplace term, even for non-techies. It was a darn household word, which is remarkable, if I do say so myself. It was 2008. The fact that you could ask someone outside of the high-tech bubble what Intel did and they "got it" was pretty much insane.

My job at Ogilvy & Mather was to leverage my start-up chops to innovate marketing for Intel Insider. I devised guerrilla-style marketing tactics, like using a brand ambassador program to get influencers to use the technology and then talk about it on video. I also put social media to good use to help spread the word in a strategic but organic way. We even partnered with Oprah for her "O Conference," which was an incredible experience (made even more incredible because that conference later inspired me to create and launch Girls in Tech's Catalyst Conference). It was no softball assignment, and it was me—a chick from the start-up world—struggling to wrangle in the bandwidth, disparate teams, and resources that Intel brought to the table. Namely, this meant roping in many different groups—social media, public relations, marketing, advertising—and getting them to collaborate and work for the greater good of the business; a supersized challenge, especially as they were working in silos to each tackle separate pieces of the program.

I'm not saying I couldn't have succeeded without my start-up experience. Who's to say? But I do know that my scrappy background placed me in a position to think creatively and innovate on my feet. *Tap dance!* My start-up roots put me in the right mind-set. *Let's do this.* It armed me with the reliance and the attitude to push harder when I felt like I was being pushed back—to simply think bigger. To come up with strategies that weren't so in-the-lines, that were a bit edgy for their time. And, at the end of the day, Intel chose to use every single one of my ideas to promote their program—a huge win for Ogilvy & Mather, a massive, heart-pounding championship for me.

But it's not just me, Tamar, or someone with start-up chops who can succeed with forays into intrapreneurship. The most appetizing part of intrapreneurship is what it can do to accelerate a company's innovation. In fact, just having time to think, to create, to brainstorm freely—well, it can result in brand spankin' new product releases, dynamite marketing campaigns, and more. All by happenstance or the desire to fix a problem you as a team are facing internally.

Take Slack, for example. It's a collaboration tool that many companies have rapidly adopted. Users can chat, share files, and discuss any topics they choose, from where to get lunch to company strategy. A lot of people have heard about Slack. But the concept was ignited by Tiny Speck, a game company that made a game, ironically, named Glitch. As I understand it (disclaimer: I've never played Glitch), the game didn't have an end point. There was no mountain to climb, no witch to kill, no spaceship to take over. Instead, players sort of wandered around, doing mindless tasks, like collecting water. Sounds a little silly, but Glitch gathered a small audience. Yet it never completely took off and was shut down in 2012.

Glitch was dead. But Tiny Speck was just getting started. They had learned something about humans and engagement and maintaining our interest levels through "boring" tasks (here's looking at you, water gathering!). Slack was Tiny Speck's foray into applying this learning to the business world. It was a total test on their part, almost playful. They went apeshit with emoticons. Added in splashes of bright color. And, of course, they had a smart-ass name. It broke rules, fearlessly tested and jabbed at users with fun chitchat and sarcastic banter.

And it drew people in. People went there to chat and wound up . . . working. Turns out, Slack was a fun place to virtually hang out in, and if you and your coworkers are already there chilling, you might as well get something done. Pure magic.

This is an example of a company pivot, but one made using an intrapreneurship mind-set: Tiny Speck gave its team time to explore what could be. It essentially told them, "It's okay to play. It's okay to experiment. It's okay to do something goofy and try something totally new. Get outside your comfort zone."

INTRAPRENEURS ARE IN DEMAND

For years, many companies have operated with the idea that "boss knows best," and some companies still do things like this. It's a bit of an antiquated management approach, where everyone is placed in a position and expected to perform specific job duties. No problem there, other than restraining a company's die-hard closet intrapreneurs, preventing them from reaching their true potential, from being satisfied at their job, and from delivering real value to the broader company. In this sense, this old approach is a lose-lose. An intrapreneur will likely grow frustrated and tired with being told exactly what to do, with following directions, and without being constantly stimulated. And a company—one that isn't progressive, that is—just won't get it. No doubt, we've all been there. So what can you do if you're an intrapreneur at heart? Start by looking for a team that will encourage, not stifle you. And as a manager or founder, there's a lot you can do to facilitate an intrapreneur-friendly organization.

Julia Hartz, CEO of Eventbrite, is a solid example of a leader who fosters intrapreneurship within her organization. Eventbrite now has more than a thousand employees, across several locations. Intrapreneurship is a core element in Eventbrite's culture of innovation and in their recruitment strategy. As they grow, they need exceptional talent, and exceptional talent needs room to run. Julia can see the theme across her candidate pool. Workers today expect more, and it's not just millennials.

"The idea of entrepreneurship or intrapreneurship evokes the feeling of freedom, and autonomy, empowerment. I think that's what people are looking for today," Julia said. "That's what we all should be seeking from our roles wherever we work. It is important for us as an organization to support that, to give people the ability to experiment and the freedom and space to make mistakes. We want to breed this feeling of empowerment because we want people to feel engaged and we want them to grow. We want them to make the right decisions. And I feel like when you're getting people to really think independently, they make better decisions versus just following the status quo."

The concept of entrepreneurship can't be discussed without discussing culture. Isn't that what this really is, a culture issue? You probably associate companies with all sorts of environments. The whole work-hard-play-hard cliché, the grueling marathon hours that happen at the Big 4 accounting firms and consultancies, the ping-pong and gaming competitions that you may link to many start-ups. Culture is largely based on company values, but they aren't the same thing. Values—honesty, integrity, accountability, for example—drive a culture. And, un-fortunately, culture is one of those critical things that many peo-ple, leaders and juniors alike, don't appreciate until it goes awry.

It's one of the things that a founder needs to guard with all your might. Bar the door. Safeguard it with your entire heart. As you grow and hire a team, especially if you're dealing with a globally dispersed team, culture can quickly become glass-fragile, a juggling game of delicate eggshells.

Julia tackles culture like an expert mixologist approaches a stiff Friday cocktail; she looks to create just the right balance in the organization, allowing for all the warm fuzzies while getting hard core when it comes to growth and innovation. Julia doesn't shy away from the fact that it's the leader's job to own her com-pany's culture. It all starts at the top, and either a founder or CEO does or does not make it a priority.

"We've created a culture that is not very political at all. We've created a culture where we win and lose together. There is a sense that it's the strength of the team. That starts to com-press the need to have people represent themselves."

Girls in Tech is a crumb of a team compared to Eventbrite (we're ten compared to their thousand!). So that drove me to ask, How do you maintain such a curated, thoughtful culture over time, especially once you hit that level of scale?

"Very carefully," Julia said. "People make choices to stop being involved in the creation of culture or being thoughtful about hiring the right leaders who are going to go on to hire the right people, or they take their eyes off the ball of what's important. And I haven't done any of that."

For large companies such as Eventbrite, this attitude allows them to move fast in ways that dinosaur corporations with tra-ditional chains of command never will be capable of. Think about how things might typically get done with an old-school approach: marketing managers have a very defined, perhaps very limited, scope. They're expected to maintain their focus on the specific projects and job duties they've been assigned; anything else might be perceived as disrespectful, frivolous even.

These managers are also expected to uphold the full chain of command. That means that they must run approval up the ole totem pole every time they want to get a lick of something done. They ask their boss, maybe a director-level type, and then the director chews on it for a bit before asking the vice president. If it passes the vice president's sniff test, it may make its way to C-level.

All of which could take weeks. Months. Efficient, no? (Please, please tell me that you picked up on my honey-thick sarcasm.)

Meanwhile, the managers with an idea or any sense of pride over a project or a problem that could be solved, what do you think happens to them? How motivated do you think they are to work harder, to innovate, to think more deeply about the barriers they may experience in their everyday? My guess is they probably don't give a shit about these things anymore. They're probably doing a game of classic clock-in-clock-out, just showing up and biding their time—until they can move on to a far more interesting and challenging and engaging experience at some other company.

And so, a culture that supports intrapreneurship must be a culture that supports growth. As a leader, that means giving your team the space to grow and to think independently. It means recognizing that sometimes things don't have to always be done exactly your way. Breathe a little; it's okay if team members want to present differently than you would. It's okay if they have a new idea about how to drive social media strategy, or run meetings, or recruit new employees. The ball is in your court to encourage self-thought. So back off, okay?

For employees to succeed in this environment, to Julia's point, they need to know they can fail, and fail with the support of their team. Does this mean you bring out the sprinkles cupcakes and send out an internal newsletter every time a project crashes and you blow your budget? Probably not an awesome idea. But this does mean you move fast and work leaner (there's a word that Silicon Valley loves!) and learn to iterate. Learn to experiment. Warm up to the notion that not everything is going to go according to plan and that it's okay to try and try and try again before you come out on top.

Companies can support this notion of failure by allowing employees to be expressive and giving them the space they need to innovate. Google may be the most famous of the tech giants to do this, with its 20 percent rule, where employees receive 20 percent of their work time to dedicate to project experimentation. This is time for employees to brainstorm, to collaborate, to create, to let ideas marinate. For big companies that have the budget bandwidth, it's an investment worth fighting for. For example, at Google, the 20 percent rule resulted in some of the company's core products, such as Gmail and AdSense.[1]

Okay, of course I get it: start-ups don't have a lot of time to spare. Despite the ping-pong visions and the happy hours, there's just too much to do. If you're a start-up founder and you have 20 percent of your tiny team's time to throw at moonshot concepts, I'm impressed. Even after more than ten years at Girls in Tech, I'm facing that same challenge: I'm working with a slim team, up against Goliath projects. This is compounded by the fact that many of our large enterprise sponsorships look to my team to execute the way a large corporation does—with all the resources, all the team members, all the budget at their fingertips. We feel the pressure, every day, to try to "make perfect" with our lean selves. This can fold into long hours and more do-it-yourself-style projects than I care to list.

For me, I try to fold in intrapreneurship concepts into project workflows, ideation, campaign management, and creative problem solving. I often find myself so busy dealing with the day-to-day chaos that it's easy to get too close to the business. It can be challenging to step back and think about the big picture and innovate when instead you're focused on fundraising, oper-ations, and building partnerships.

And so I count on my team to do that thinking for me. I lean on them to think about what bigger things need to happen so we can make a win. I lean on them to look at Girls in Tech with fresh eyes, to ideate, to create new concepts (and to slow me down if that's what it takes to catch my attention and get things done. *Catch me if you can.*) I know what direction we need to head in, but my core team drives the boat and charts the course—and that means keeping the organization afloat with fresh concepts and bright ideas.

Tamar and her "brags" idea is a perfect example. I also turn to a slew of consultants and contractors to guide me. So maybe intrapreneurship, then, is also a *trust issue.* For an organization of any size to foster intrapreneurship, you must—*absolutely must*—trust your employees implicitly. If you can't do that, then you're hiring the wrong people.

Intrapreneurship can unfold by your design as a founder. I seek to create a foundation for intrapreneurship within Girls in Tech despite our extremely limited resources. Each Monday we start our week off with a "Weekly Sprint" meeting; it's an intrapreneurship spin on the old-school staff meeting. Sure, we touch base on where we are with major projects. But we also have coffee, and we bullshit and brainstorm and scribble and whiteboard for at least one to two hours. Imagine a freestyle approach to team meetings. The point isn't to waste anyone's time (we ain't got time for that!); it's to encourage connecting, laughter, new ideas.

Another thing I do, and I've done it this way since before Girls in Tech: every team member receives a free-wheeling journal. It's not meant to be cute; it's meant to be a total mind sponge, a place to soak up ideas generated on the fly, in or out of the office. A place to draw and to dream and to imagine. I'm a hardcore journal carrier. If we did one of those street interviews where you ask me what's in my purse, I'd proudly pull out my journal and show it to you.

And finally, I also make the resources available to the organization readily available to my team. Need to run something by a board member? No problem. Want to learn how to code so you can experience it? Sure, let me make a phone call. We may be limited in our capital and our traditional resources, but we're amazing at making do with the resources and gifts that come our way. We take them and run.

Run. Freedom. *Total permission to explore.*

GET COMFORTABLE WITH BEING UNCOMFORTABLE

Julia recognizes that, from an intrapreneur's standpoint, having this level of freedom and trust may be a bit uncomfortable. But in her mind, for anyone to experience massive growth in their career, discomfort serves as a trail marker that you're doing it right.

"The feeling of discomfort is a signal that you are growing and that you're doing the right thing by challenging yourself and pushing yourself," she said. "This goes for people coming up in their careers or those building entirely new companies."

Are you an intrapreneur who is flirting with the idea of real entrepreneurship? Are you toying with the idea of starting your own company? If so, I encourage you to give some thought to whether you have what it takes, and whether you're willing to put in the commitment and time a start-up baby will take (circle back to Chapter 1, "What It Takes"). How will you know whether you should take that leap from intra- to entre-? If you increasingly find yourself daydreaming about what it could mean to have more control in your career, you may be an entrepreneur. If you hate slowing down to match the pace of your company, you may be an entrepreneur. If you're crazy resourceful, accustomed to getting shit done and taking charge, you might be an entrepreneur.

But you'll never find out for sure unless you take the plunge, right? Just do it. Remember, real entrepreneurs have no fear of risk and failure.

WHAT DID WE LEARN?

✓ **Intrapreneurship benefits your team and your start-up.**

Companies are pretty darn shortsighted if they think that hiring a leader in every individual isn't going to pay off big time on the back end. Don't you want a company of doers? You want people who just get shit done for you and who update you on the way. Aiming for anything less is the equivalent of cutting off your own arm.

For employees, they get to work at a place that respects their individuality and supports them so much that they won't want to go anywhere else—they're going to want to stay and thrive and take off on your turf. For companies, they get to accelerate the pace of business and reap all the benefits of innovation. Intrapreneurship should be a pillar of your culture, not by happenstance but by choice.

✓ **Let go of your inner control freak.**

Yeah, I know, I'm a huge drag. Way to ruin the party, right? Entrepreneurs by nature can be born control freaks, and, at first, that's something to celebrate. You're in control of your destiny! You're in control of your product plan! Of every line of code, of every design decision, of every hire and partner. You're like a chess master in the throes of the game, moving all the pieces and dictating every direction. But, as you grow, this can no longer be so. You've got to let go if you want to reach for the stars.

✓ Make time for creativity.

If you can, carve out time every day or every week to be creative and freestyle your job, either solo or with your team. Think about how you'd improve things if you didn't have to run projects up the decision pole. Consider issues you're experiencing within your work or your team—how could you resolve them? What tools do you need to overcome them? Or an alternative approach would be to just not think at all. Whiteboard and scribble and let your mind sort of relax. All these strategies will help you come back to your real "job" feeling renewed, refreshed, and armed with a new perspective.

✓ Get comfortable with feeling uncomfortable.

This is for both sides of the equation. Whereas founders may need to get comfy with letting go, intrapreneurs need to establish and test their own limitations, their own decision-making prowess, their ability to ideate and run with projects end-to-end. A lot of people can't do this—they need direction and hand holding. Constant reassurance that they're doing things okay. But when fear or doubt strikes, intrapreneurs (or those learning to become intrapreneurs) should look at it as a learning opportunity versus a test. And then embrace it with everything they've got.

CHAPTER 4

Business for Good

OUR VALUES DETERMINE the decisions we make in business. Our values determine our culture. Whereas intrapreneurship offers a culture with the space to innovate and take charge, what about your broader business values? How do you want to leave the world a better place? How will your start-up affect generations to come in a positive way? How do you want your employees to operate in a global economy? These are all things you must consider on the front end, though hopefully building some "good" into your business feels organic, too.

"I've always done stuff with good intention. From a very young age, I was obsessed with how can I do good and make money at the same time? Thirtysomething years ago that was considered kind of crazy. And now, thank goodness, it's the norm," said Vicki Saunders, founder of SheEO.

SheEO is a movement, very much grassroots, founded by Vicki and headquartered in Canada. Her goal is to empower women by funding female entrepreneurs. Five hundred women, who SheEO refers to as Activators, put in exactly $1,100 each. The money is then loaned to five separate female-led start-up ventures, under the agreement that the loan will be paid back in five years.

But this isn't any typical fund, venture or otherwise. It's what Vicki refers to as an "act of radical generosity." The loan pay-backs feed into the master fund and then get loaned out, again, to yet another five female-led start-up ventures—perpetually. The goal is to go on forever, in this nonstop domino-style giving train, where women all over the world can join forces to lift each other up by helping other women succeed.

It is crazy. It is radical. And it is working. This is global, do-good social innovation at its finest.

The five hundred women Activators pool more than their money. They advise the start-ups. They buy from the start-ups. They use their vast networks to connect the start-up to the resources it needs to soar. SheEO is on a path to onboard one million women Activators and create a fund of $1 billion to help 10,000 women. That's worth celebrating.

And Vicki does. You can hear it in her voice, glowing through the phone, and see it onstage when she presents. She's spoken at Girls in Tech's Catalyst Conference, where she takes over the room with her bold idea, her determination to change the world and kick down doors for women, all through gen-erosity. I've seen her speak, and I've seen people in the room look up, a spark being lit within them. Vicki is a mind shifter. She's the saleswoman who convinces people not just to buy into SheEO but to come running, checkbook open, pen at the ready. It's not a marketing scam or impressive speaker training (the woman doesn't need it); for Vicki, this concept lives in her heart, flows through her veins, is exhaled and inhaled with every breath.

She's in the business of doing good. Right where she belongs.

She told me that she once heard a definition of entrepre-neurship, one that has stuck with her since. It was in a book called *Disclosing New Worlds*, by Charles Spinosa. She said it "talked about entrepreneurship as history making. It was an act of citizenship almost, in solidarity with the world. That just so resonated with me. It was this broad, beautiful definition, what are you here to change and to make your mark in the world? That is the lens through which I've looked my whole life."

We've talked a lot about what draws entrepreneurs in— what about the start-up world, in all of its rough and tumble landscape, really does it for entrepreneurs, the ones who wind up doing something versus just talking about it? For many it's natural. An urge to fix something. A call to go their own way, to forgo the rules, to break down walls. Very few of the people I've spoken to for the book (any?) have mentioned money, though if done right, entrepreneurship will get you there.

Vicki said she views entrepreneurship as her ticket to business freedom. You run the business, you do whatever you want with it, assuming you're not burdened by the rules of a public company, of course. You get to make money. Reinvest it in your team. Contribute back to them or give the money to the community you serve. You're the head honcho—and you don't have to be a dick about it. You have a choice to do something thrillingly wonderful.

And this idea—of doing what you want and following your purpose and just simply being YOU—it takes courage. You have to march forward and dismiss the doubters, Vicki said; surround yourself with a tribe of people who will support you and see you through.

"We live in an environment where most people are not reaching their true potential," she said. "It's a challenging, unforgiving world. Living in our world is hard, period. Then, taking a dream that may be outside the norm of what people are doing and then stretching yourself to achieve that is this huge courageous act. So, my favorite people to be around are dreamers and doers and entrepreneurs who say, 'I want to achieve X.' And just go for it. That's radical. That's awesome."

(*Pssst*—I just have to point out that Vicki mentioned entrepreneurs who "just go for it." See, there's that fearlessness again,
that impulse to just get things done versus overthinking it. It's
like this happy, fear-free, sizzling productivity virus that takes
over each one of us.)

Yet. We can't do it alone. We can't reach the top all by ourselves. Vicki pointed out that, especially for women, it's not
natural to ask for help. That makes many of us feel uncomfortable. Inadequate, even. And so many of us start out with this
grand potential but then "get cultured to be smaller than we
want to be."

Which can be lonely. Isolating. And completely against the
SheEO model of women helping other women. This led Vicki
to wonder, in the earliest days of SheEO, when it was an idea
racing through her heart, whether she was onto something
real and whether people would do something so revolutionary
rather than just talk about it. To figure this out, she did something startlingly simple: she just asked.

When she speaks, she asks the room, "How many of you
will help?" Everyone's hands go up in the air. And then she
asks, "How many of you would ask for help?" and no one's
hands go up. Nope, women don't like asking for help. To ask for
help—to be vulnerable and in need and to admit that you need
something or someone—it requires boldness. Jumping through
a fire.

"You have to get over your fear of asking," she said. "Once
you start to ask, you literally have everything you need around
you. That's part of the lesson. The only way to not feel alone is
to reach out, but that's hard to do."

Vicki had to do more than ask a room, however. She had to
see whether her concept had wings. For her earliest testing, she
began with ten women who put in $5,000 each. They looked to
support super-early-stage, pre-revenue tech start-ups; they created a little mini-incubator of sorts and doled out a grant, rather

than a loan. But then Vicki thought even bigger: she turned SheEO into a perpetual fund instead; she wanted start-ups to repay the money. So, start-ups have to have at least $50,000 in revenue to apply to SheEO, which gathers $500,000—but it's up to the five start-ups to split it among themselves, with two rules: the money cannot be split evenly, and it cannot be given to just one of the start-ups. The founders need to get in a room, open up their books (just days after meeting!), and maximize that $500,000 within the group, however that ends up looking. Often, this means they power together—sharing strategies, pushing back, brainstorming ideas. It's an intense level of due diligence, but "they walk out like they have formed a new sisterhood." And they'll receive SheEO funds at a very low interest rate and then pay it back to fuel generation after generation.

Vicki tested this idea again in her speaking engagements—an early, simple, free way to run her concept by many women at once. She said that women would come up to her after speaking and ask to write a check on the spot. *Just tell me who to make it out to.* People jumped at the chance to help. And this happened over and over again. And then Vicki knew—she was onto something. And so, she went with it. She stepped off that bridge and took that risk.

"There's a ton of moving parts. There's a million things that could go wrong. Yet it's all working out."

If I've made it sound easy, that was not my intent. Vicki is still up against many challenges in her pursuit of that $1 billion fund. The biggest remains the transaction-based mind-set that has been burned into so many. The idea that there needs to be a direct exchange. You have money. You put it in. You get it out. SheEO crushes that; it's a global network of trust and faith. People are putting in $1,100, and the path before them is uncertain (ring a bell?). That can make some people squirm. That's understandable; it's just not normal to throw more than a grand into a giant pot and *trust*.

But Vicki insists that now is the time. The time to trust. The best time to be a woman. And the time to make these radical changes.

"I think being a woman right now is a massive competitive advantage. We see the world differently. We understand relationships. We're moving away from a transaction-based world to a relationship-based world, where humanity is at the core of this. . . . We need to show up with our dreams and support each other."

START-UPS + GOOD VALUES = DOING THE RIGHT THING

Okay, so why are we talking about SheEO and business for good? In a grimy start-up book?

It's important to open your eyes to the changes that are sweeping across the business world. Not everyone these days is trying to build the next Trump Tower and rake in the big bucks and count their pennies and exploit the powerless. You can be an entrepreneur who makes money and does something good. You can call the shots, have the flexibility you so desire, and change the world. Yes, *you*.

Many people link the millennial generation with inspiring change; this group of people wants to work for companies with values that align with their own, with a mission greater than turning a profit. Millennials are said to care about causes. They want to feel good about their work. Yet Vicki is not a millennial, nor am I—proof that anyone can and should aim to drive business for good.

Tech often drives start-ups. People get into the start-up world because they want to build something, they want to launch this or that product. To create. Yet Vicki said she's looked at tech as an enabler rather than as the core of any one of her businesses. Girls in Tech, although a nonprofit, operates in very much the same way. We're the gel that connects the female

STEM community with high-tech companies and start-ups. We often use technology to *get things done*, but Girls in Tech was not formed to *create* technology. (I'm no developer!) For us, it's just another tool in our kit of connecting women and providing a career launchpad. Technology is our yellow brick road.

It's not a requirement by any means, but entrepreneurs today have more room than ever to do good with their business. This can be radical generosity like Vicki's, a start-up like Girls in Tech, or something even simpler. Have the courage to consider what your true potential is? (No pressure, right?)

Don't overthink this process—start with your ethics. Begin by making good, smart decisions. I'm talking about putting a human behind your customer service policy and not being that founder who screws people over. It can start with your brand promise, just being the type of company people want to work with, because you're a good human and so are your people and so is your brand. *It starts at the top.*

Moving up a level: an easy do-good strategy is to link up with a charity of choice and to share your earnings with that trusted partner. Or, heck, even form your own charity or fund or internship program. The idea is to feed back into your community and share your success with others. *Lift everyone up.*

You can also choose to do good by thinking about the type of business you're creating and the value it offers the greater community. How can your business transform people's lives for the better? How can your business educate, uplift, and inspire? Think about what causes you feel personally connected to or about how your natural skills or business model can be leveraged to make a difference, not just a buck.

Are you making healthy food more accessible—easier to access, cook, store, and serve? Are you eliminating chemicals from our diets? Are you educating people? Are you connecting subgroups of people within communities, in a way that is beneficial for all? Are you helping mothers who have been out of the traditional workforce, as stay-at-home-moms, to regain regular employment?

Think about what you would be doing if you didn't have to work for the money. It sounds a bit cheesy, I know, but where does your imagination take you when you consider that scenario? Every business can do good and serve communities. Look at Airbnb. Their business is about putting butts in beds and helping people to find affordable, interesting, and unique places to stay . . . or is it? They aren't perfect, don't get me wrong. But they are also about enabling home owners (and RV owners, tent owners, comfy couch owners, and retrofitted garage owners) to become their own version of a B and B host. Yet they also have helped victims of disasters, such as Hurricanes Irma and Maria, to find shelter when theirs got swept away in floods and ravaged by fire. They've leveraged their network and their business to lend a hand to people who have absolutely nothing to give back. *Shelter, a basic human need.* Brought to you by Airbnb.

Because it's the right thing to do.

What a fascinating thing, to help others in the age of digitalization. There are so many alarming headlines across the media and cynics on every corner who lament the fact that we're all growing apart from each other. No sense of community, children on video games all day long, who knows their neighbors now? No one picks up the phone anymore.

But perhaps this business for good trend is a sign that, no, we haven't lost a sense of community and we sure as hell haven't lost each other. We don't pick up the phone like we used to (*text me, don't call, okay?*). But we've picked up powerful applications instead; we've connected with neighbors online— perhaps far more readily than we would have embraced them just a few decades ago.

We've become people who find babysitters and senior helpers through technology. We share our homes and our cars with each other. We reach out and date online when it seems like there's no one to have dinner with. We're innovating technologies that our societies have been built on, such as construction and farming, to make for a better world. We're using technology to communicate instantly about what we're putting into our bodies, what products we're using on our children. We're using tech to enable a wave of political reform—ripples of petitions and direct communication with your local representatives.

No, you don't need to launch the next Girls in Tech or SheEO to pat yourself on the back and check the "I Did Good Today" box. But I challenge each of you, readers, to consider how you're going to incorporate something good—something right and true—within your start-ups or at your current company.

It can be done. It needs to be done. Let's all be better to one another, shall we?

In the words of my first mentor: no excuses.

WHAT DID WE LEARN?

✓ **We may be conditioned to think smaller, to stick within a conventional box.**
Do we get funneled into certain boxes? Programmed over time to perhaps dream a little less, stick closer to home, find a career with the comforts of stability and convention? Maybe. After all, it's safer there, to live within the lines, isn't it? Ask yourself what your true potential is. It's a scary thing to do, looking at yourself in the mirror (or, if you're like me, muttering to yourself on a commuter train). Because you have to be honest and that's tough to do. But maybe it's time to have the conversation with yourself about what you want to be doing, what problems you see in the world and how you—you!—can begin to fix them.

✓ **Sometimes all you have to do is ask.**

Who doesn't want to be Superwoman? I don't know a single person out there who would turn away that amazing retro belt, flashy cape, and all the powers that come along with them. Yet here we are, trudging through the world, in a crowd of so many, feeling so alone. But the truth is that other women are here and willing to help you. Asking can result in a wave of support and impact and joy for both parties. Go on, give it a try.

✓ **You can always do good (no excuses).**

I don't care whether you're on Wall Street or you're hammering a piece of hardware technology at your kitchen table. You can do good today and do good every day with your business. How can you just be a better person and help your community? Ask yourself what you have to give and what your business can give. Be realistic. You're likely to be surprised at the creativity and flexibility captured within your response.

PART II

*

On Start-up Essentials

CHAPTER 5

On Stress

WELCOME TO THE Start-up Essentials. Stress belongs in the Start-up Essentials section, not because it's necessary but because it's inevitable. Stress, like every topic in the Start-up Essentials section, is unavoidable. There's no way you can squeeze past this sucker. It's a part of the package you sign up for when you go the start-up route. Just like with my rant on being a woman in tech, I want not to discourage you but to prepare you for what's to come. If being a woman in tech is complex, stress can be an even darker web. Good thing there are coping strategies you can put to work, which I'll share later in this chapter.

FALLING APART

It was a Thursday night when it first happened. I was about to step into a delightfully steamy hot shower at my home in San Francisco, and, in preparation, I yanked out the tie that was holding my dark hair back.

Out with it came hair. A lot of hair. A *chunk* of hair.

It lay there on my vanity, dark and menacing against the shiny white quartz backdrop. If you didn't know it was my locks and you turned the corner to enter my little city toilet, you might think a small rodent crawled up the side of the sink to take its last breath. You might even scream and grab a broom and dustpan, thinking a good beating is required before the ceremonious flush down the waterways to heaven.

But nope. I knew it was my hair. And I stared at it with all the horror a midthirties female would. No, let's try that again. I stared at it with all the horror a midthirties human being would, especially one who had to *show up at a conference* in just a few months, shake hands, *meet people*. Face to face! You know, hopefully with hair on my head.

It happened again—three times—which means I went to see my general physician for answers. She wasn't in the room with me for more than two minutes when she said, "It's stress."

Internally, my eyes rolled. Who isn't stressed out? Who doesn't have a lot going on, especially in San Francisco? Externally, I took a deep breath. I pulled together a shiny smile. And replied, sweetly, "Stress? I was thinking it could be a nutritional thing, you know, I read something about—"

"No, it's stress. This is a classic physiological response to severe stress. Your body is sort of shutting down, and shedding hair is a sign of that. And I can even tell you, just at a glance, you don't seem as healthy as you typically do. You're pale, and you look tired. Is something going on in your life that could be causing a stress response in your body?"

I couldn't pretend everything was okay, not anymore. No, I wasn't sleeping. No, I wasn't eating, not enough. I went through each day with a softball-size knot of anxiety in my stomach. I was working too much, and I was experiencing halo-style headaches that gripped me in throbbing pain for hours. At least every other night, I'd climb into the bathtub—my attempt at unwinding—but I couldn't dump enough salt in the tub to work out my woes.

It was that check—remember that damn $95K check for my first big conference?—and the burden of it, combined with an event that was just months out. It was almost too much to bear.

See, money is my kryptonite. I worry about it—even now, years later, when Girls in Tech is in a far more stable place. It's a constant worry. And when I get these stress episodes and when shit really hits the fan, there's a good chance money is involved in some way.

It's not a greed thing, it's a reality thing. Girls in Tech *needs* money to survive. I *need* money to survive. The organization *needs* money to pay people. It goes back to the whole concept of fueling yourself before you can fuel others. It's a stark, raw, scary side of business because money, or a lack of it, holds power. It has the power to shut the lights off completely. It also offers the power to open the most grandiose of doors.

For all the cute things people say about money not buying happiness, I can sure as hell tell you that it does in fact buy reliable hair—and shit tons of peace of mind.

Stress eats away at every entrepreneur. If you've seen the iconic *Silicon Valley* TV show—starring Amanda Crew, who has been a tremendous supporter of Girls in Tech—you may remember some scenes from the first season where Richard, founder of Pied Piper, the fictitious start-up featured in the series, repeatedly sees his doctor for stress-related checkups.

In one episode, Richard explains his latest start-up drama to his doctor. He's grappling with a tough decision: Should he accept an offer to be acquired? On one hand, he walks away with a boatload of cash. On the other, he walks away from his vision and his dream.

"You know, a while back, we had a guy in here in almost the exact same situation. Take the money or keep the company?" the doctor says to Richard.

"What happened?" Richard asked.

"Well, a couple months later, he was brought into the ER with a self-inflicted gunshot wound. I guess he really regretted not taking that money."

"He shot himself because he turned down the money?" Richard asked, incredulously.

"Or no, he took the money. Or no . . . he did not . . . you know what, I don't remember. But whatever it was, he regretted it so much that he ended up shooting himself and now he's blind. Just FYI, if you're ever going to shoot yourself, don't hold the gun up to your temple, okay? It just basically took out both of his optic nerves, and then half of his face. And then his wife left him, because, you know, yikes. He may have been a genius programmer but not so much in human anatomy. Or decision making for that matter!"[1]

Although the episode is admittedly hilarious—especially Richard's shocked reaction—there's a dark, raw truth to it. Stress is a *real problem* in the start-up world. And it's something that is very hard to relate to or understand until you have your own start-up; it's completely unlike the "oh, I just had a shitty work week, I seriously need a happy hour or a day of sleeping in" sort of stress that busy corporate environments may invoke. There's a deep intensity to start-up stress. Every decision brings with it a bitchy layer of intensity. Things can get heavy, fast.

THE DARK SIDE OF START-UPS

Here's the thing with stress. We all know it's happening, but not everyone talks about it outright. It's like a secret drug habit that is only a secret to those on the outside. I've had friends that have had movie-category nervous breakdowns—total hysteria, complete body shutdowns, moments of trembling panic and anxiety.

I've had friends wind up in the ER because of heart palpitations. Night sweats. They're talking in their sleep, crying through nightmares.

I know people with regular panic attacks. They're experiencing so much pressure that they snap like a no. 2 pencil. Decisions can lead them to tear up.

And therapists—let's just say they're in high demand in NorCal.

The stress over that $95K check caused me to go into hiding and to recede into a place within myself I didn't know existed. As a founder, you spend so much time investing in something—in the building of it, in your dreams for it, in your vision for all it could be. It's like your child. When it doesn't work, it's pure tragedy.

To date, that time was the most trying experience of my life because it tested who I am at my core. I thought I was a good negotiator. In fact, I thought I could talk my way into (or out of) almost anything. When that initial e-mail came through—after I was done with the semiautomatic string of F-bombs that shot through my brain—I had the arrogance to think, "No big deal, I'll just talk to them. They'll make it go away." After all, I was a good persuader and it would be a piece of cake . . . wouldn't it?

It's a funny thing, admitting that you lost it. Loony bin lost it. On the outside, I have a polished outer shell. People tell me I'm charming. I like to dress nice for work. I date nice men. I throw dinner parties with bubbly and live mariachi bands (I'm Mexican, what can I say). I make homemade chili rellenos, and friends always ask for seconds.

I work out. Hell, I'd go as far as to say that I'm the niche entrepreneur who has the discipline to carve out time for herself. I take care of myself. I go for runs. I book myself to see shows and concerts, guilt-free. At a glance, I live a balanced, happy life.

But one of my better skills is that I'm a warrior when it comes to compartmentalizing stress. I treat it like a travel T-shirt and roll it up swiftly, shove it into a cute little carry-on, and jam it into a dark corner within. Here's a pro tip for you readers: You know that thing they say about internalizing stress being bad for you? It is.

Don't do it.

During that chaotic time, my parents once again became my pillars. They damn near became my employees. I gave them access to files and set them up with e-mail accounts. They came through for me in a way that no one else did. They took on the mundane—calling vendors, performing research, handling social media. And they took on the mammoth projects like navigating the event agenda and reviewing presentations.

My lack of a partner during this time heightened my stress. It also heightened my doubt. At least fifty times a day, I'd wonder how I would pull it together. People came out of the woodwork—people I had never heard of—asking for money. Designers, photographers, and others were suddenly knocking on my door, yet there were no contracts. There were verbal deals in place that I didn't know about, and they were coming due. But I had nothing left to give.

TOTAL BURNOUT

Lisa Falzone, founder and former CEO of Revel Systems POS, a mobile payments platform, knows stress. She started Revel in her twenties and grew it to about seven hundred people—that's massive growth for a leader of any age. She's observed what she calls a four-year burnout period for start-up founders. She described how, as a young first-time founder, the stress snuck up on her and resulted in numerous physical manifestations.

"I underestimated how much the stress can build up," she said. "I started Revel when I was twenty-five. I wasn't really self-aware about how much the stress was getting to me. I ran Revel for six and a half years. I've spoken to a lot of founders, and it seems like year three or four, you hit burnout. I definitely hit it around that time."

Here's what that looked like for her: She just shut down. Literally. "I had heart palpitations. I had a bad back, but then my back got really, really bad. It's kind of a side of entrepreneurship that no one really talks about, just how much the stress can affect you, physically and your health. It's so common, and you start really getting to know different entrepreneurs. Almost everyone I know, if they're honest about it, has gone through extreme burnout around year four. Your body can only be under extended stress for so long. If it's chronic stress, you can only really handle that for a couple years."

Lisa said she sees this three- to four-year burnout across most entrepreneurs she comes across in her circle. For her, it started out of a lack of awareness, but it was also veiled in guilt: she had to constantly work to feel like she was moving the needle and that things were getting done and the company would make it to the other side. She was so head down in her business that everything outside of it was on the back burner.

If I wasn't working until late at night, it felt like we wouldn't survive. You have to at least partially reprioritize your life and realize that health is important. I was so singular[ly] focused. I didn't put a lot of emphasis into friends and family. I ignored a lot of relationships for those four years. Not purposely; I was just so focused, I didn't make time for it. I didn't make time to develop a spiritual practice, or meditation, or anything to keep [me] more self-aware.

I see a lot of my story in Lisa and vice versa. The physical shutdown. Becoming reclusive. Being obsessive about Girls in Tech. All these things that have so much upside—the grit, the hard work, the long hours—are a double-edge sword.

It's so easy to slip and get cut if you don't establish boundaries.

GETTING TO THE OTHER SIDE

So, here we are—I obviously survived that first Catalyst Conference; I've lived to write this book, haven't I? The conference itself went well.

It took me a few days to come up for air after the flurry of madness. I was amazed. *Holy shit, I can actually fundraise. I pulled it off.* I did the one thing we all need to do to sustain a business: get money. The thing that overwhelmed me the most, that scared me the most, that makes me bite my nails and causes my hair to fall out—I faced it and I won. Not only did I raise enough to cover the costs of the Phoenix conference, but I raised a big fat cushion that allowed Girls in Tech to keep humming forward. I was floored. And I did it on my own, which was like a turbocharged boost to my confidence.

I realized that companies *want* to support Girls in Tech. They see the value in the organization. Despite my doubts that I told our story well, I communicated Girls in Tech's value proposition in such a way that people got it, they nodded yes, they reached for their checkbooks. I realized that I could count on these companies to be my partners in execution. That conference established the roots of our current fundraising strategy, where we rely heavily on corporate sponsors to achieve our mission. It was something I always knew, but having it unfold so magically before me felt like an epiphany of sorts. *This works. They'll pay for this.* I can't say it enough: it was a really big deal. That was how I started working for Girls in Tech full time.

When I think back on it now, I still feel the glow. Attendee responses echoed the energy I felt in those coming days. We received a tidal wave of overwhelmingly positive feedback from attendees. These e-mails and evaluations were music to my ears. When I didn't think I was going to pull off the conference, I had originally planned to focus on self-care and recovery, but, instead, I was celebrating our praise. I felt an invisible link to these women who wrote to me to say their lives had been altered.

I know what I want to do in my life now, and I know I'll be attending future Catalyst Conferences. I want to get involved in Girls in Tech.

The conference was so inspirational to me. I'll never forget the women I met there.

It was so amazing to be in a room with so many influential women. I don't feel like I'm alone anymore. Thank you for doing this!

I could go on. The notes that rolled in were genuine and heartfelt. They acted like a thermal recovery blanket for my heart.

But the stress of start-up life never goes away, and it's never tied to just a single event. My most challenging time now, the thing that sticks with me every day and every week, is managing my team and helping it retain focus. As CEO, I need to help my team feel a sense of urgency. I need to set milestones and nudge things forward, bit by bit. Sharing this sense of passion and urgency is tough to do with people who aren't you who aren't so deeply intertwined into your mission (no matter what amazing employees they are!).

And money. It's still a problem. I can't sustain a staff, hire more people, drive programs forward if I don't have money.

Girls in Tech is an odd bird when it comes to finances; things are at once simplified and deeply complex because of our nonprofit, do-good nature. We're always walking a fence with budget—how much to give away versus spend at the corporate level, what's appropriate for an event budget, how to retain sponsors for longer periods, rather than just for one-off events.

This yearning for balance hangs over my head. I can't shake it, nor should I. It's more about how I manage stress and think through these challenges. Since that $95K fallout, I feel I've gotten better at creating life strategies to help me manage the stress that is inevitably a part of my lifestyle.

As I mentioned above, I'm good at *making time* for myself. And when I say "make time" I mean it—you must make it, guard it, treasure it. And, yeah, setting boundaries can be a bitch. Here's how I do it: I block time in my calendar for me. I make commitments that are difficult to untangle from, by involving other people—paying for a yoga class ahead of time, making that massage appointment that I'll be charged for if I don't show up.

I also physically strive to get away, at least once a month. It doesn't have to be a sexy jaunt to Europe; a drive to the sea or to wine country will suffice. Physically removing myself from the bounds of the city clears my mind and allows me to perform a mental reboot—something that is just not possible when I'm home.

I'm also a big fan of rising early. I don't rise early and jump right in front of my laptop; rather, I rise early and just be. I'll meditate if possible, even just for ten minutes. I'll also clean my house, sip on coffee, and take my time embracing the day ahead. By the time I roll into the office at 9 A.M. sharp, I'm ready to rock. I'm prepared, rested, and eager to take on the day, whatever it might bring.

I really don't know what most days can bring. So I try to not worry about it so much. It's one day at a time. One week at a time. And, through it all, I'm trying (still trying) to take care of me along the way. I can't say it's a habit yet, but I do know one thing. I'll shove you like a four-hundred-pound linebacker if you try to get between me and my massage. Just sayin'.

WHAT DID WE LEARN?

- ✓ **Don't underestimate the stress.**
  I mean it—don't be the fool who thinks you're going to be the one entrepreneur who manages to escape its grasp. It will get to you, it's just a matter of when (according to Falzone, it'll be about three or four years in). Know that it's coming. Mentally prepare for it. Know what to watch out for: relationships falling away, not eating, not sleeping, racing heart. Anxiety is about the simple decisions.

- ✓ **Make setting boundaries a habit.**
  Do it even when you feel like you have your shit together. Make it a habit to go out for lunch instead of eating at your keyboard; indulge in the joy of zoning out, say, with a book, a mindless TV show, or a day's getaway. You can even fold stress relief into your workday by doing things like taking meetings over a walk. It's no substitute for alone time, but it sure beats rotting away for fourteen-hour days in an office.

- ✓ **You're not alone.**
  There's this funny underworld "fight club" thing that happens with entrepreneurs. We're all going through the same puddle of mud, but no one wants to talk about it. Ah, the battle of being the eternal optimists . . . talking about it

would make it too real, too much of a downer, right? Well, maybe that needs to change. Confide in another entrepreneur friend if you're going through a tough time. Have a talk with your cofounders, and tell them what you're dealing with. Do it over coffee, over lunch, or over the phone. If it's someone you trust that you can be vulnerable with, go on and have a cry. It'll probably feel good.

CHAPTER 6

Partners

NOW THAT THE cat's out of the bag about start-ups' ugly, stressful side, this is a good time to bridge into the topic of cofounders, or partners. These people can ride the highs and lows of your start-up right alongside you. Having someone to lean on, for many of you, may be reason enough to find a cofounder. The trick is finding the right one.

Partnering with the right cofounder takes a lot of due diligence and a little luck. A lot of people say it's like marriage. And I suppose that's true in some regards. Marriage can be about romance, unconditional love, and vows. And start-ups offer the adrenaline high that often accompanies romance: the flirtatiousness of spontaneity, the cement-like bond that team members feel when they're surfing the highest wave or trudging through the deepest shit. In either instance, you're in it for better or for worse.

I've spoken to a lot of entrepreneurs about cofounders. It's a polarizing issue. It doesn't seem like many entrepreneurs flounder on this topic. Most believe that you need cofounders, period. You're not going to get ahead without them. And a lot of founders fall into this by sheer luck. I've known some cofounders who have met each other in the crowds of innocent San Francisco happy hours, those who have coupled up at co-founder meet-and-greet events, others who have met through friends. In an ecosystem such as Silicon Valley, you can meet your cofounder at the corner Whole Foods. Nope, there's no huge secret society, folks. Cofounders often fall together be-cause a group of people are at the right place at the right time. Alcohol often helps the process.

I'm sure there's also a "safety in numbers" mentality. This whole start-up thing, it's frightening. Perhaps it's more fun to know you have that partner to cry with, to laugh with, to cel-ebrate with. To lose hair with. Joining forces with a cofounder from the start provides a built-in buddy system. *We're in it to-gether. We're stronger together.*

Not me. I go it alone.

I'm all for team sports, but I'm also for clarity, for owner-ship, and for taking charge. I think a lot of people pair up with cofounders for the wrong reasons (namely, fear). The challenge with linking up with randos on an idea that is *yours*—one that runs through your blood, your spark, your genius—is that they aren't *you*.

I don't think there's any issue with claiming it as your own, your baby. I believe that no one will ever be as committed to a business concept as you. When it's your idea, when it's your dream, your passion, your baby—it's *all you*. You are the heart-beat. You are the brand. You can try your hardest to convince others of your vision. You can inspire them, draft them for your wild ride. And, sure, you'll come across quite a few who will pledge allegiance to your idea. But you're *it* at the end of the day. No one can replicate how you feel about it. No amount of equity percentage is going to make people feel as you do about your start-up.

There's something about being first. About being the starter, and I don't think it can be replicated.

This isn't to say that you shouldn't, or you can't, *share* your big idea. In fact, I would argue that you must. If you think you're going to build something worthwhile alone, that's laughable. You may be the chief architect, but you still need others to help lug the stones and set them in place. I couldn't do this without my team. There's too much to do, too much to focus on for one person.

So, yes, pull in other team members. Surround yourself with brilliance, with a team of people you trust who can be founding *members*. Gather an army and onboard them to help you achieve what you started off to do. These will be the people you work late with, toast with, pitch with, sell with. These will be the people you sweat with and rely on. They'll be your start-up family. You should be hiring people you know who will take initiative. This is your first opportunity to foster an environment where intrapreneurs can soar.

Look at some pretty well-known companies, and you'll see that I'm not alone in my loner approach. Take Jeff Bezos, the one founder of Amazon, a company you may rely on for just about every aspect of your day, from streaming entertainment to groceries and diapers and bar soap. He's built the empire that we all can't live without—and he did it as a solo founder. But he didn't do it *alone* by any means. As soon as he had some funding (a million bucks generated by VCs), he focused on hiring technical talent to build his dream, which in those days meant savvy coders who could sling out web pages in C+.

Sure, solo founders are rare. But many founders seek cofounders because they feel like they *have to*. A lot of newbies view finding a cofounder as a checklist item. They don't even consider doing things on their own. Skipping over this idea is shortsighted.

Mark Suster, a venture capitalist based in Los Angeles, notes that the idea that one absolutely needs a cofounder is deep rooted in start-up wisdom: "So embedded is this conventional wisdom in Silicon Valley that it feels like heresy to even question it. It's a sacred cow, for sure."

He continues, "Conventional wisdom says that you gain far more in working as a team than you lose by diluting by half before you start. Conventional wisdom doesn't account for all of the things that go wrong in partnerships over time; especially ones that are formed quickly and without a long gestation period."[1]

On the contrary, Clara Shih, CEO of Hearsay Social, told me, "There is an indescribable amount of work that goes into starting a business, and especially in the early years, every day is an emotional roller coaster. For me personally, there was no way I could have gone through this alone, and I feel incredibly grateful to have cofounded Hearsay with Steve Garrity, a close friend I had known since we were freshmen at Stanford."

I've always been on my own with Girls in Tech, largely because I've never bought into the idea that I absolutely need a cofounder. Now, of course, I realize I'm never truly on my own. The organization in its entirety—aside from a modest handful of corporate employees—is operated by a grassroots style, volunteer army of remarkable women. No, I'm not on my own in that sense. But I am on my own in the sense that it stops with me. It's my name behind the Girls in Tech brand. I'm the one pounding the pavement for corporate sponsorship dollars. I'm quoted in the press, and there's only one person listed as founder in the "About Us" section on the website.

Being the sole founder has its advantages. I get to make decisions freely (pending board review). I get to play out my vision, the one that runs through my own head, for my private viewing only. These two benefits cut out a hell of a lot of drama, decision-making time, and hassle. The decision-making perk, in particular, can't be downplayed. So many start-up founders bicker over the most mundane choices. And what happens? Total paralysis. Nothing gets done, the whole deal just becomes one giant compost pile for recycling one crappy decision-making conversation after the other.

Yet, with anything, there are drawbacks to being in it alone. "Alone" can be a shitty word. Alone. If the organization tanks, guess what? It's my name that's linked to it. When the board has a question, I'm the only one there to answer. For important events, such as last-minute meetings or a press interview, I'm a lone wolf standing, looking for help. There are a lot of nights I work late; it's just me and my Mac cranking things out until 2 A.M. I'd be a huge liar if I told you it didn't get a bit lonely.

Cofounders. It's a personal decision. What's right for me may not be right for you.

Just know this: your cofounder could be the element that gives your idea wings or makes it tank in spectacular *Titanic* fashion (minus the violin music and gaudy jewels). When the team is as tiny as two people, it doesn't take much to make it soar or make it tank. There's nowhere to hide if you're fighting. There are no other voices in the room if you disagree. You're betting that 50 percent of your company or thereabouts will be safe in the hands of this cofounder. That's high stakes for a party of two.

Cofounders, though, can provide you with a secret ammunition that can be hard to stockpile in the caverns of Silicon Valley: confidence. You'll see that I talk a lot about confidence in this book. In fact, I've dedicated an entire section to it. *It's that important.* Cofounders mean you've got a wingman or wing-woman who will accompany you for both the darkest and the most exhilarating milestones of your journey. When you want to celebrate a win, of any kind, be it making a hard-to-achieve connection to a VC or receiving news that you've been awarded your first seed check, you've got a built-in buddy system for celebrating. When you don't know the answer (as you won't most of the time, at least in the very early stages), you have a familiar face to turn to. When real life happens, such as emergencies, a sick kid, a parent in the hospital, you have someone else who can at least temporarily keep things going. And you know that person will care for your baby just as much as you would.

On the flip side, a relationship with the wrong cofounder will quickly breed resentment. Spats over who is working enough—competitions over the hours spent or not spent. Bratty comments about connections, money, and priorities. The worst cases tend to include a tug-of-war over silly decisions, things that seem so big at the time but are so tiny in the long run, like e-mail format or brand colors. It's a game of power plays and treading water. I've also seen plenty of disagreements stem from dishonesty—as in cofounders not being honest about what workload they are truly capable of or what strengths they bring to the table. It never ends well.

But sometimes it does. Let's take a look at warm and fuzzy, shall we? Cara Delzer, one of three founders and CEO of the San Francisco–based hardware start-up Moxxly, the maker of a new and improved breast pump, is a great example. She kicked off the start-up full time with her cofounders, who were just finishing things up in their graduate programs. Delzer had a brand-new baby and a full-time job when she decided to take the start-up plunge and look for cofounders to join her journey.

Her story is one of bliss, the start-up romance I'm sure so many of you are reaching for. For Cara, finding her cofounders felt organic and natural. She even compares it to meeting her husband and just knowing he was the one.

"It's like getting set up on a blind date and then agreeing after a couple of dates to get married," she told me. "It really is a marriage or a long-term partnership. My cofounders and I joke about the coffee meetings that we had in the beginning. And it really is awkward. You're trying to understand, is this a smart and good person that I should sign up my professional future with? I only met this person thirty minutes ago." Cara goes on to describe how meeting potential cofounders involves a lot more than just talking about business plans:

And then there's all this sensitivity in the early part of working on an idea [and] on sharing your idea and what you want to do [and] the insights you have. It's a dance, what do I [say about] what I think this should [become]? But how do I also show that I am committed and smart and creative. It's just this funny dance. If you're founder dating and looking for people that you don't know that aren't in your network, there's probably no way around the awkwardness.

It worked for Moxxly, and it was a lot like when I met my husband. I just knew, right away. It felt like that with my founders. The best way I can describe it is, we were sort of having two conversations at once. The first was: well, I think there should be a better breast pump. And I have these skills to help make it better, and I have these skills, and so on. We were talking about solving the immediate problem.

But, on the second level, there was this sense of possibility around the brand and what this could be beyond just solving the breast pump product problem. With that, we were just sort of alike in our sense of humor, and what we thought those brand values could be. We had a very similar vantage point on the opportunity. It felt like we had been talking a lot longer than we had.

Now, like a lot of great love stories, the Moxxly cofounder one is rare. Dating can also feel exasperating, lonely, and pointless. When you're single, it seems like no one is ever a good fit, and the excitement of dating can fade fast—likewise with finding the right fit in a business partner. No, it's not always effortless like Moxxly—in fact, it's rarely as easy and more often hard as hell. Here's where you can take another clue from dating: ask to be set up with someone. Just like it helps to be linked to other singles when you're dating, it can be very beneficial to ask everyone you know in the start-up world to connect you with an appropriate cofounder; it's a no-nonsense way to let others in. But, remember, when you go in business with another person, you always take a risk that you're doing a deal with someone who doesn't share your values (you know, like meeting someone at a bar and saying, "I do" before you get to know each other).

And finally, when all else fails in dating, pull out your phone and use an app! Technology has facilitated the cofounder experience. Meet-up groups, networking events, and websites like CoFoundersLab and FounderDating accelerate the meet-and-greet process. Like a job recruitment platform, now you can search for the skill sets you need, the location you need, and even outline what you're willing to share or give up with your cofounder, namely, equity. If you are truly set on a cofounder, be prepared to ask questions—a lot of candid, intimate questions—before getting serious.

Ask about their work style. Their strengths. How they think through problems. Where they like to work, what times they like to work, who they may have connections to. Ask them about what's going on in their personal lives—are they able to commit their emotions, finances, and time to a start-up? This is the time to be brutally honest with yourself and with your potential partner.

WHEN COFOUNDERS FALL APART

As for the dark side of cofounders . . . well, as much as Delzer had a whimsical experience in finding her cofounders, Darrell Mockus, one of the original engineers at Match.com, had an unfortunate one. In the late '90s he was cofounder of a start-up called e-Vangel, which offered technical due diligence services for venture capitalists.

"My business partner was going through a nasty divorce. I was on the short end of a stick," he told me. "And I lost everything." Details aside—when he lost everything, he means *everything.*

He now offers this advice to those of you who are seeking cofounders: "I would highly pay attention to their personal situation. For example, if someone is going through a divorce, I can tell you, just stay clear of that one. Those are very hard personal situations. And you're talking about someone who you require 85 percent of their personal time to dedicate toward your company. They're not going to be able to give that to you."

Darrell also suggested you investigate a cofounder's personal financial situation before joining forces. This is where you need to be okay with asking the tough questions. Do they have money stockpiled to get through the ups and downs of your start-up? And for how long, specifically? What are their financial needs, how much debt are they in, and do they have an unrealistic salary expectation? What is their plan for surviving if they wind up needing more personal cash to stay afloat? If you see warning signs that your potential cofounder can't last for a few years and doesn't have any extra padding in his or her budget or a partner (say, a spouse) to help support the start-up lifestyle, then it may not be a healthy situation to commit to.

"Also, you want to make sure you have the same interests in solving the same problem," Darrell advised. "Personally, I would have had no interest in doing something like Pinterest. I still don't even understand it! I would have been a horrible CTO, because I don't believe in it."

What Darrell is really saying is this: money can only take you so far. You and your cofounder must be jointly cemented to your start-up idea, and not just for the sake of putting "Founder" on your business card. At some point—and that some point is pretty damn early on for a start-up—both cofounders must believe that all the hard work, the late hours, the exhaustion, is worth it. If you're working on something that either of you feel is even just a teeny bit silly (in Darrell's case, a photo-sharing website) or you don't even "get it," then your runway of tolerance is going to be too short to allow for any success, period. Move on. If you don't, you'll be forced to move on because your lack of passion will show up in your work. Your cofounder will ask you to move on if it's you, or you'll be put in a position to ask your cofounder to leave. Bottom line: it won't end well. Make sure you and your cofounder have equal passion for tackling the same problems and that no one is just going through the motions.

Being honest with yourself, and your needs, extends to every aspect of the founder-cofounder relationship. There's a lot of ways to slice the pie. Think creatively about what your needs are and what will best fulfill them. Anu Shukla, of RewardsPay, is a big proponent of cofounders or, at the very least, founding members. But she pointed out that you need to be very clear on who is what and who has decision-making authority (being a founding team member is different from being head honcho). And Jessica Scorpio, from the car-sharing start-up Getaround, was candid that she and her cofounders didn't have an equal split in the start-up—and that is okay. In Scorpio's situation, not all founders started full-time at the same time. Not all founders had equal responsibilities. Scorpio stresses that you need to take a hard look at what each founding member brings to the table—how much time that person can commit, what his or her skills and background are—and have a candid discussion about percentage equity you think each member should receive.

No, it's not all equal. Things are not sliced and diced in exact portions. No, not everyone gets an equal say.

The result more closely mirrors fault lines or the clumsy cuts of a blindfolded cake-cutting contest. Life is not fair, and start-up life sure as hell isn't either.

WHAT DID WE LEARN?

✓ **You don't necessarily need a cofounder,
but you do need help. You can't do this alone.**
Come to this realization—fast. You. Can't. Do. It. Alone.
This could mean partnering with the right folks or delegating. But, either way, get over the idea that you're Superwoman. Focus on your vision and how to best achieve it.
Open yourself up to the idea that you may be an odd bird in
Start-up Land. Maybe you want to fly solo; maybe you want
a few cofounders. But just remember that—unlike what a
lot of "experts" tell you—there's no right and wrong.

✓ **Consider the type of person you are, how you
operate, and what your needs are as an organization.
Where are your gaps? Figure that out first, then hire to
close the gaps.**
I've heard this time and time again: fill in your gaps. Nothing
new, right? But it takes a huge bite of humble pie to make it
happen. You need to admit where you're wrong, where you
fail, where you're weak. As hard as it may be, facing these
challenges head-on may lead you to the greatest successes of
your life. For me, I've always struggled with delegating. Girls
in Tech is so close to my heart, it's gut-wrenching at times
to dole things out. Even if it means getting things done in a
far more efficient way.

I'm going to tell you an embarrassing, ugly secret. Here
goes. As recently as last year, I lost sleep over the idea of
hiring an admin. I couldn't do it. Many people told me I
needed one. And I knew I needed one—but I was so used to
being on my own and doing so much by myself, I couldn't
bring myself to find someone right for the role. I was doing it

all, from presentations to scheduling meetings—and killing myself in the process. I fought hiring help, even to the point of using an AI-powered admin for a few months (fun at first, until my meetings got screwed up and there was no one to call). The idea of counting on someone was that hard for me to chew on, to the point of stupidity. Sometimes you have to let go in order to move forward.

(Yes, I have an incredible admin now, and, yes, I'm kicking myself for not having hired help five years ago. Argh!)

✓ Cofounder relationships don't have to be an even 50-50 split.

A 50-50 split is the obvious, but why does it have to be 50-50? If both parties are not contributing to your venture equally, they should not be compensated equally. This applies to work and relationships. If one cofounder is extremely well connected and opens up one door after the other, for example, then he or she should be compensated for that—even if they're working fewer hours. It's about deliverables.

✓ Evaluate cofounder candidates with your eyes wide open. Look at their personal situation. Are they in a decently healthy financial situation to be able to take the risk on a start-up? Are they emotionally stable? Do their life circumstances support a commitment to start-up life?

Start-up life isn't a vacation. Don't treat it as such. It's not a short-term commitment. Look your other team members in the eye, and ask yourself whether you can deal with them for at least five to seven years. Are they stable enough to ride out the turbulent times with you, or are they distracted on the home front? If you have any doubts whatsoever, walk away.

If there's one thing you take away from all of this, I hope it's that you need to have the courage to do what's right for you and your start-up. There's no prescription for the cofounder relationship. There's no script to follow.

No doubt, most start-ups seem to have at least two or three cofounders. But don't overthink it. You need to be brave enough to carve your own path. It's complex and intimidating to do, especially when you're new, but just know that it's okay to go rogue. It's okay to go it alone, as long as you can bring on the right resources to help you succeed.

(But take it from me. If you need an admin, hire a human, not a robot.)

CHAPTER 7

Advisors

WHEREAS COFOUNDERS BRING with them a risk of disaster, advisors offer the opportunity for total warm fuzzies. Advisors are all about *you*—as you'll see, you get out of them as much as you put into the relationship.

If you surround yourself with the right advisors, the lessons they teach you will stick with you for your lifetime. One of my first lessons came from Maria, a woman I reported to when I interned for a local Los Angeles media and advertising company the summer before I graduated. I reported to Maria, and she was a manager to many. Your managers throughout your career also serve as your advisors, informal or not. For me, a young, earnest chick on the brink of graduation who still didn't understand basic business acumen and who simply showed up every day trying to do her best, Maria was it for me. And, for that time in my life, she was enough.

I took cues from her behavior, the way she breezed into the office with such confidence, her heels clicking as she strode across the studio floor. Assistants and subordinates often walked alongside her during these micro strolls, leaning in to try to get a word in or to receive a go-ahead nod of approval for a project. Maria was Latina, she was in power, and she wore a dress with such comfort, it was as though she was wearing cotton jammies. She was my idol.

Of course, I observed all of this mostly from afar, from my humble intern desk, crammed into a studio corner. For the most part, I was on my own. I performed tasks that most managers wouldn't lose sleep over, like filing, responding to general studio inquiries, running papers to this office, and things like that. Sometimes I would fact check, translate content from English to Spanish, or join in a team brainstorm for a new marketing program.

But, one day, Maria asked something slightly more important of me. She needed me to get some signatures on some urgent documents—I'm not sure what they were, it was all a sea of legalese to me—but one thing should have been clear: she needed me to hustle, fast.

I also don't recall the specifics of where or how I dropped the ball, but I did drop the ball. I didn't get things done in time, and I know it affected the launch date of a major project.

"Adri, can you bring those signatures to my office, please?" My old-school desk phone buzzed with her request.

"I'll be right there," I replied.

I made my way to her corner office with the papers I did have, the signatures I did gather. I was missing two, but at the time the importance of the whole thing didn't resonate with me. In fact, I don't recall being upset that I hadn't completed the ask, or ashamed in any way.

When I arrived, I handed her the ones I had gathered so far.

"I should have the others tomorrow," I said. "Probably in the morning."

Her face fell. That's one thing I remember, the way it just fell. Disappointment. I saw it on her face and then felt the shame spread through me.

"You don't have them? I needed these. By *today*. So we could put in the advertising order." She didn't sound quite so angry as she was shocked. Her fresh-faced intern had failed her.

"I'm sorry. One person was out of town, and I tried calling the other and I just haven't been able to get through. I've called three times," I said. "I'll try again right away in the morning when their office opens again."

She sighed. "Listen, I don't want to hear excuses. No excuses, okay? I should have heard about this sooner if you were having issues getting people to sign off."

No excuses. No excuses. That's the lesson that I haven't been able to shake, and it's been twenty years since she taught it to me. It's the one thing I catch myself telling my own team when details get dropped, a sponsorship deal doesn't close, or an event doesn't unfold according to our vision. No excuses.

I share this story with you to underscore the role these advisors will play in your life. Who would have suspected that a lesson learned through an internship would have stuck with me for a lifetime? Throughout your career, you'll find yourself with many mentors and advisors. Respect and value these relationships, even if they seem minor in the present. You never know what you'll take away or how long their wisdom will stick with you.

Most of these relationships will not be formal in nature—advisors and mentors are the people who tuck you under their wing and make sure you don't get sidelined in the corporate world; they're the managers a level or two higher than you in the chain of command who take a special interest in your talents and see that, yes, you should get to participate in that resume-dazzling project. They're your parents, your friends, the people you connect with at networking nights—and stay in touch with over the years because you realize you have common threads in life. Advisors come from all walks. They each serve their own purpose in steering you in the right direction. That's what makes them so valuable.

Now, in the start-up environment, advisors tend to take a more formal role. You still have the friendlies that I mentioned above, but now you've got an advisory team to deal with. These are folks that you count on early in your start-up for advice. They may have contacts you need. They may have niche industry advice, and you want a front seat inside their head. At any rate, you need them more than they need you, and in return for their contacts, advice, or even seed funds, they'll likely expect to be compensated for their time.

Fran Maier, a cofounder of Match.com, talked to me about being an advisor at a time of transition in her life. She was evaluating her next move: she had just purchased a house in San Francisco, and her sons were graduating from high school and college. It was 2012, and Fran had moved into a neighborhood where the hot new start-up Airbnb was just down the street from her. Her new home had its own bedroom and bath on the top floor, and she figured—why not be a host? Travelers flocked to her home in droves, and, while she figured out a groove with her new lifestyle as an Airbnb host, she decided to advise some companies, as well.

In 2013 she did a keynote speech at Women 2.0, and she realized she had hit a niche audience of hungry young women—new founders or those interested in starting their own venture. That speech became Fran's foray into the advising world. For her, it was simply fun.

"Advisory relationships for companies can be very helpful," she said. "You really have to do it because you really want to help, not because you think your advisor shares are going to be worth a fortune. And, if you think the company is really going somewhere, you're probably going to be making some investments. At some point, you become an investor and not an advisor."

Fran admitted that when she first started advising start-ups, she had her door wide open to requests—she was perhaps overly generous with her time. She was advising almost anyone, but then she became more discerning. She shifted gears to focus only on companies where she truly thought her skill set could be helpful, companies that really spoke to her.

"I advised companies where I saw that the CEOs will listen and were coachable," she said. "It's a lot like angel investing. From an angel investment standpoint, you want to look at the founder, the market opportunity. You want to see if the founder is coachable; do they have a network? What are the skills they bring to the start-up? Your time is like your money. In a lot of ways, you need to look at advising relationships with that same lens."

She noted that she ran across a few companies that would ask her for advice—but would fail to send her the paperwork. This was a sign to "not waste your time," she said, a red flag that the start-up founders aren't serious or aren't organized enough to get the ball rolling.

And that ball—it is on the founder to kick it into motion. Fran looks to her start-ups to ask questions, reach out, and engage her in what they need. She typically advises on marketing strategy, pitch deck, overall value proposition, how to raise money—a broad range of topics. She said advisees also look to access to her network, but this can be a bit sensitive.

"There is sometimes the expectation that [founders will] make you an advisee, and you'll not only advise, you'll invest and introduce them to all the investors you know. It doesn't really work that way," she said. "I've got to know a company pretty well and know there's a strong fit with potential investors. It's not like I'm going to go and open up my whole LinkedIn."

However, it is helpful, Fran noted, if entrepreneurs peruse her LinkedIn and explain why and how they want to be connected. She rarely will ever give a straight up intro. She'll typically ask the person who is the target of the introduction whether they're open to being introduced, purely as a common courtesy.

And so founders need to own the relationship in full. Advisors may look for 0.1 to 1 percent (give or take) in exchange for their time and expertise. They are not getting paid in cash, so leverage these advisors carefully, and respect the boundaries they set. Better yet, have a plan with your advisor before you enter a formal relationship. Get clear on what you need from him or her, how much contact you want, and exactly what deliverables may look like. (*Pssst!* A good rule of thumb: the more traction your start-up has gained, the lower the percentage an advisor would receive, and there's typically a vesting schedule of two to four years.)

THE BOARD OF DIRECTORS

Next up: as you grow and hopefully get funded, you'll be forming a board of directors, an even more formal set of advisors. Your board is responsible for governing your organization. They make decisions on critical matters, such as fundraising rounds, overseeing you as the founder, and guiding the overall direction of the company. The board is an important component of your start-up, and if you work with your board members wisely, you can get a heck of a lot of value from them. But managing your board can potentially be one of your biggest jobs as a CEO, something that catches many first-time entrepreneurs off guard.

You may be very comfortable being in the weeds with your start-up and focusing on the daily grind, but now you have this entirely separate group to manage (beyond your hired team, of course). This means managing ideas, varied interests, and, potentially, politics. Board members have skin in the game, and they will have a say about how your company is managed. It's in their best interests to be involved in your organization and to help you navigate the challenges you'll inevitably face as a founder.

Coco Brown is founder and CEO of the Athena Alliance, an organization formed to bring more women and more diverse roles into corporate boardrooms. She coaches, mentors, and prepares remarkable women leaders to take board seats. I'm grateful to Coco for sharing so many of her talented members with Girls in Tech when it comes to conferences and other events. It's mutually beneficial: Coco's Athena members get visibility and public speaking experience, and Girls in Tech gets access to rock stars. A win all around.

Because Coco's career is rooted in board diversity, she's an expert on how to work with boards and set them up for success. She noted that, as a start-up grows and continues to take on investment money, founders may find themselves with dwindling control. Over time, it may be less about who you want on your board—and your specific picks—and more about investor's picks. You may get who you get, and this person is very likely to be a white man.

"If you're going to take that [investment] money, you will end up building a board with more than just you and the people you elect on it. It will have investment representation on it. Over time, the balance can be more investors and fewer of you and your founder(s)," Coco said. "You don't want 100 percent women on your board. But you want balance, you want diversity."

So, how can you retain some sort of balance, even while your company grows and your investments grow? Coco suggested that founders tackle the diversity issue early on, at the investment deal stage, and become intentional about their plans for a diverse, well-rounded board. She suggested talking to investors and putting it in writing, while deals are still being carved out, that the board representation needs to be 50 percent female and that, as partners, you will collectively work to see that happen. Write it in as part of the deal.

Another aspect to consider when you're being intentional about your board is what you can expect to receive in exchange for a board seat. Of course, with investors, you're getting money as part of the deal. But what else can you expect of them? How much time can they dedicate to you, how often do they want to meet (or can they meet), and what resources do they have that they're willing to share with you? These resources may be personal resources (such as industry knowledge or contacts) or resources that their organization can bring to your start-up. It's up to you to ask these questions and set these expectations, long before board members get too comfy in their seats.

For example, Coco has a board member she meets with weekly for an hour. He offers her tremendous value because he has such a deep experience in boards. Because he has seen so much, he's able to fast-track discussions, guide her in other ways to approach challenges, and can even provide templates for specific documents she puts together.

"He's become my sounding board around long-term strategy and planning," she said. "That's what he's willing to bring to the table."

Now, when it comes to managing your board and working with it as a team in the best interests of your company, try to take a thoughtful approach. Coco noted that you must be aware that you're wearing a few hats. One, you're the founder. Yup, that means the board can fire you. Remember, you report to the board, so you're a bit vulnerable. Another hat you wear is that of peer on the board, meaning you're a member and you may even be chairwoman. When you think of it this way, you're a true peer, and you need to drive the board to be the effective and impactful tool it should be.

To be successful, you must ground yourself in both roles. You also must form individual relationships with each board member, something that takes time and effort. Don't wait to talk to board members until the quarterly meeting rolls around.

Here's where Coco said many of us go wrong: "We tend to default to the role where the board is superior to me. This can happen very quickly because we bring very powerful people onto our board, which is great. It can be really easy to fall into this place where we report to the board as opposed to 'I am a peer in this board,' particularly for first-time founders."

Another challenge is keeping the board on track and maintaining focus. Coco suggested that, as a team, you agree on the top metrics that the board will review together every single time you meet. But it's not just about making a list of metrics and checking the box. For founders, preparation is key. You must consider what questions the board will ask if your metrics are off or if you're behind in your goals. Put yourself in the board members' shoes and make sure you have data points to back up your metrics—every time. Make sure you think through answers to their potential questions—every time.

Having the answers at your fingertips isn't just to make you look good; it's to keep the conversation hyper-focused. Make the metrics portion of the meeting consistent. Review the top metrics, answer questions, and quickly get into alignment about what you are (or aren't) going to do to change them. In this way, you strategically rally the board to maintain focus and be more effective as a group. You're in control.

This isn't where the preparation stops, however. Coco noted the other potentially windy aspect of board meetings is the strategic discussions—the brainstorming, the what-ifs, the conversations that can potentially meander and crush a meeting. Her suggested fix? Frame these strategic questions well in advance of a board meeting. Ask every member these questions ahead of time, and ask them to come prepared with their response, ideas, or advice. This avoids discussions that can lead to nowhere, and we've all been there. Lots of brainstorming, lots of ideas, but the meeting ends and there's no clear resolution.

Intimidated yet? If so, that's understandable. The idea of managing and collaborating with powerful board members is certainly daunting. But it's also okay to show your cards a bit. Don't be ashamed to ask for help and to call attention to your lack of experience. For one, they'll get it—board members realize they aren't working with veteran founders every time. And, second, by pointing out that you're a first-time founder, you're explicitly calling attention to the fact that you may require more guidance and mentorship. Flat-out ask for it. Let them know you need it—and that you expect it!

Say it:

> *I need mentoring.*
> *I've never done this before.*
> *I need help with this.*
> *I need a coach.*
> *I would like your support. I need more support.*
> *Can you provide more guidance here?*

Get comfortable asking for help. Get cozy with admitting to others that you're not perfect (yeah, yeah, yeah, I know that's difficult to do).

Here's a little secret, are you listening? Coco said many women don't ask for these things enough. "I can tell you, I see male CEOs doing it all the time. And I see women thinking it's a luxury they can't offer themselves. It's amazing to me. And men think nothing of it."

A lot of this comes back to confidence, to having that *fuck it!* attitude and being able to ask for what you need, without apology. (Stay with me, I talk more about confidence later in Chapter 10.)

Girls in Tech has a formal board. Of course, these members aren't on the board in exchange for money, because we are a nonprofit, but they are on the board in exchange for their dedication and ability to help facilitate the right connections for the organization and to drive support where needed.

I've always had loose advisors for the organization throughout the years, but I formalized a board in 2015. It was time. I was going full time myself, I was developing a more strategic approach to fundraising (you know, after my breakdown over the $95K bill), and I knew I needed some sort of structure in place if I was going to scale this puppy.

For the early days of the board, I made instinctive decisions. From the gut, not a lot of analysis, fast. I turned to those who I had already naturally been turning to for some time; I turned to people in my network who seemed to show up, who were relentlessly reliable. The ones who had proven themselves over the years, even in a less formal capacity. I also asked newbies, and I'll be candid: these were people with impressive brand names behind their titles, people who seemed interesting in helping but who didn't have much to show for it.

I wish I could say that every single one of them worked out. But no. A lot of people are more interested in *saying* they are on the board of a global nonprofit than truly *participating* on one. A lot of folks wanted to update their LinkedIn and say they're a Girls in Tech board member; they wanted to mention it in the whispers of their networking circles, receive looks of praise and the proverbial pats on the back; but these individuals didn't want to come through when it came time to promoting events or helping me form the right connections for the organization. Often, I felt vulnerable. I was told—not just a few times—that they could probably help raise money for us or get their giant brand behind a lucrative sponsorship opportunity. Then these things fell through—more than once. A lot more than once. And it would make me burn inside to see these members tout being on our board when they did pretty much nothing.

However, over the past few years, I've become wise to the problem. I've done some much-needed shuffling, and now I feel like the team is solid. Of course, it's far easier for me to switch up my board than it is for a funded start-up board because there's no equity involved.

There are a few standout board members who have stood out as people I can trust with Girls in Tech business or personal issues. Remember, this is my *baby*. One woman has truly absorbed her role as board member and has become one of my greatest confidantes: Sandy Carter, vice president at Amazon Web Services. This chick is my mentor, my role model, my friend.

I've turned to her for a range of issues—governance, finances, staffing, events, how to deal with partners, you name it. She never sugarcoats her advice, which has built trust over the years, yet she remains emphatic throughout every interaction. One thing I noticed is that she asks me, "How are *you* doing? Where do *you* need support?" She's consistent about these things. She shows up when I need her, and there's a lot to be said for that.

I feel deep singularity with this woman. She serves as an example of the kind of relationship I hope to foster with every board member, where I can call them any time, they consistently come through, and where I can ask them anything, and they'll give me a straight answer every time. Look for the people who will do the same for you.

BUILDING THE RIGHT CONNECTIONS

Would you be where you are today without some sort of connection? In the job that you're in, or at your start-up, or speaking with this or that investor? Most of us get to where we are going with help from someone in our network. But where most of you may fail is that you think it needs to be an intimate connection to ask for help.

You don't have to be best friends. Just ask. You'll be surprised about who offers to help.

"Connections have been instrumental in helping me make the idea better and helping find the right people to bring the idea to life," said Jessica Herrin, founder and CEO of Stella and Dot, the massive direct-marketing community of women who sell the brand's clothing, jewelry, and accessories.

Herrin knew she needed help on the direct selling and jewelry side, in bringing her idea to life. But talking about her business and reaching out to total strangers also taught her a lesson in feedback: she needed to learn to accept it. She needed to learn to not be offended, to just listen. She said she considers it an art, the ability to listen to someone else's thoughts with an open mind.

But how do you build your network and expand your Rolodex of connections? Don't overthink it. It doesn't have to be about business card exchanges and awkward meet-ups. If you're truly passionate about your start-up (remember, you and your cofounder[s] must be doing something that you're crazy about), then you should just be able to open your mouth and talk about it.

"It's really [about] going around and talking to as many people as you can about the business. . . . I've often found entrepreneurs make the mistake of being top secret. Honestly, if the only thing that stands between you and your business succeeding is you having a conversation with one person, you've got bigger problems."

For Herrin, what really helped was asking her business school network.

People were willing to make introductions. I started my first business out of business school, and that was very helpful. People were willing to talk to [me]. Often it was a favor for a friend. What I had to do was ask everyone. Who do you know that knows something about this or that?

I just asked around. I posted on message boards. "Who do you know?" and randomly someone connected me with who is now our chairman of our board and an investor. But that was because I posted on a message board . . . and on the jewelry side, I found someone through my husband and his class reunion and telling people what I did.

By the way, this is what I love about San Francisco—people are willing to help. I told you early in the book that it took a few attempts before I stuck to the city. But this attitude and willingness to help others was a large part of what did it for me. In a city of innovators, it's relatively easy to find someone who is willing to listen to you and lend you a hand. So open your mouth and speak, woman! Everyone is iterating in San Francisco—their life, their career, their start-up. Everyone is on a constant experiment. Everyone is grappling with a problem.

When you share yours with an open mind—willing to receive feedback—you may be surprised at who extends a hand, a connection, a resource. I've gotten everything from free office space to investor meetings from just talking about what I love best. People invite me to conferences to talk. They ask to sponsor events. They connect me to influencers without me asking. And it's all because I talk about Girls in Tech constantly, not to be obnoxious but because it's *on my mind*. It's natural. And guess what? People listen. Corporate sponsors fall in my lap because they hear me out and want to help.

So, the key to being a world-class networker, readers? It's just talking. And loving what you do. The two should go hand in hand and be easy and natural. If they are, everything else will fall into place.

KNOW WHO YOU CAN LEAN ON

Outside of boards and advisors and random connections, you're going to need a circle of trust. For me this role falls to old friends or fellow founders. Frankly, I've found that some of my close guy friends often do the trick. They tend to cut the bullshit and just give me quick answers and nonjudgmental feedback. I'm a woman, and I can't deny that some women can overcomplicate things; we tend to inherently overthink situations. But the way many men present advice is slap-in-the-face logical. Simplified. That's exactly what I need in moments of stress. Sometimes you don't want the craft cocktail with fresh seasonal fruits and cute umbrellas. Sometimes you just need the shot of Patrón. Often, for me, it can be found in the advice of a man.

And reaching out to others where the buck stops never hurts. Founders. CEOs. This can be a lonely position to be in, and there's a built-in level of trust and respect, a soldier-like regard, that we hold for one another from the start. I know many founders who regularly meet for happy hours or power breakfasts with other founders; there are CEO meet-ups and things of that nature. Being in the room with those who are undergoing the same level of stress, similar challenges, nonstop pressure, it helps.

I'll take it all. I'll take the support whether it comes in a board seat, parental hug, or friendly phone call. Yes, I am a feminist. Yes, I am a founder. But, no, I'm never going to be exclusive when it comes to advice and supporting one another. I know I need all I can get, and I'm happy to dole it out, too.

WHAT DID WE LEARN?

✓ **Ask for help.**
A-ha. It seems so simple, but this is where so many first-time founders go wrong. They create a board, check it off the list, but don't use it to its full potential. Look, your board is not a to-do item. It's not a cute start-up accessory. It's there to serve you and to help you build a business. Your board members are like gems sitting in velvet-lined boxes; they're there to be used! Ask them questions, fill them in on where you're weak. They can fill the gaps, or they'll know people who can help you. Better yet, they'll save you a hell of a lot of mental anguish overanalyzing all the time. Lean on them, and kick your ego to the side in the meantime. That's what they are there for.

✓ **Manage expectations—before people become advisors.**
This is where I've screwed up: not creating formal expectations before extending board offers. Don't make the same mistake. Before bringing people on as advisors or board members, let them know what you need and expect—the frequency of meetings, the kinds of support you need, the level of commitment. Get it in writing. If they seem hesitant or like they can't commit, ask them who can.

✓ **View your board as your peers.**
This flows heavily into a confidence discussion. Your board members may have impressive titles, they may be older than you, and they may have a sexy lineup of companies sprinkled across their resume. But you're in charge now. You're founder and CEO, damn it. Enough with the imposter syndrome. You deserve to be here, you deserve to be sitting on your board right alongside them. Act like it.

√ **Talk about your start-up.**

It sounds simple, but I realize it also takes courage. Talking about your start-up will lead you to a surprise network, just by discussing what you love on an airplane, at the coffee shop, in class, at your pitch events. It doesn't matter where. The only thing that matters is your attitude and your willingness to share. These things will, without a doubt, lead you to people who are curious about you and want to help you in your pursuit, simply because it's the nice (or intriguing) thing to do. It's one of the most delightful surprises about humanity and innovative ecosystems like San Francisco.

√ **Find those outside your organization you can trust.**

You're not an island. No one expects you to get with your girlfriends on a Friday night, paint your toenails, and sob to each other. But you do need to reach out and find some sort of reliable support outside the formalities of your organization. Give someone you trust a phone call and run a problem by him or her. Tell a friend, or your parents, that you're having a shitty week. I'm guessing they'll welcome the opportunity to help squash some of your distress with open arms.

CHAPTER 8

Building Your Team (Thoughts on Hiring)

PARTNERS AND ADVISORS are terrific, but you also need an army by your side, helping you execute. This means you need a team. Easier said than done.

Look, I turned to this chapter with a skeptical eye. I didn't know whether to run to it and tightly embrace it—*I needed you!*—or fight it off with a stick. I even struggled with whether I should write this chapter at all, because including it meant that I would have to own up to something. *Publicly* own up to something. *Gulp.* That is, I'd have to tell you that:

I suck at hiring.

There ya go. Okay, that wasn't so bad. I'm terrible at hiring. In fact, the whole team-building, hiring, retaining-people thing has been a struggle for me in its entirety. Just saying it makes me feel a bit cagey because leaders are supposed to be world-class recruiters (right?). But building my team has been something I grapple with, jiujitsu-style. Everything starts off smooth and friendly, but with some relationships it's turned downright icy. It's messy, emotions sometimes get involved, and, yeah, I wear my heart on my sleeve. So, there's that.

Now, recruiting, on the contrary, that's one category I freakin' excel in. And I attribute that to the rise of the Girls in Tech brand. If the Girls in Tech brand were an old car, I'd be the crazy broad polishing it in my driveway every evening, proudly and protectively buffing away every fingerprint. Making it shine just so, grinning when twilight passersby admire my elbow grease. The brand is my baby, and it's grown (thrived!) organically: no fancy Madison Ave. firm required.

So, when I occasionally post the open Girls in Tech job, we get resumes flowing in. Fast. Without fail. It's part of the beauty of community, of grassroots effort. The mission calls to women around the world; it speaks to them. They want to get involved. I pay attention to this. Finding people who have a passion for making a difference, who truly care, that's part of the battle in the nonprofit world.

Because—as I've said before in Partners, Chapter 6—no one is going to care as much as the founder. No one.

But finding someone who is excited about making a dent in the mission? That's a good next step. And I've got it down pat. I'll point out that I'm lucky that Girls in Tech has a solid pipeline of sponsorships these days, to help hire these amazing people. Recruiting is tough shit when you have almost nothing to offer. Up until just a few years ago, I operated pretty much entirely on volunteers and my own pocketbook.

Now, my failure on the second half of this equation, the actual hiring post-recruiting efforts—well, I'm still figuring that one out. It's an area I know I've grown in, yet an area that I'm learning. I've yet to find my way. Perhaps I move too fast— too fast to make the processes that should be in place by now to support robust recruiting. Maybe I'm not onboarding in a textbook manner. Maybe, just maybe, I'm moving too fast altogether. Too fast to slow down and really connect with my team when they need it.

Okay fine. I'll cut to the chase. Girls in Tech has been known to be a bit of a revolving door.

Here's the deal with hiring in the nonprofit world. To be the right fit as a candidate, a can-do attitude is required. You need muscles and brains and a willingness to do the yucky work as well as the strategic dreaming. Knowing this is one thing. I post jobs, but I often find referrals through my friends, Facebook community, and partners. I'm proud to say that working for Girls in Tech is something that many people get excited about.

I hire fast. I don't have time to stroll through the process. I make knee-jerk decisions (and not always right ones) based on my intuition and the first few interviews. We're a small team at Girls in Tech. A tiny team! I'm pressed to get the hiring portion done so our productivity doesn't wane. Because of this, and because chemistry and trust count more than anything on small teams, a lot of people don't last.

New hires start with enthusiasm. I start with trust. It's a deal breaker for me. Because we're such a small team, it's important that we get along, trust one another, and know that we're all going to be accountable for our pieces of the mission. Somewhere along the way, between months one and six-ish, things sometimes get muddled. Balls get dropped. There may be personality conflicts. There's confusion over who owns what.

It's like our team dynamics short-circuit after a very short run of it. Something is going wrong, and, because people don't last, I link it to the hiring process. I'm just hiring the wrong people. And then I'm failing them (Argh! That hurts to say.) as a leader.

To combat this, I'm cutting back. Big time.

Last year, I decided I traveled too much (yup, there is such a thing). This year, I cut back on that dramatically to help make

things smoother on the home front, both at work and personally. It's not fun going around the globe when you're getting
sick all the time and you're just flat burned out. I'm optimistic
that my additional time spent in San Francisco with the team
will help in creating more unity. I want to get to know the people on my team better. I want to help them fill in the gaps, to
know where they are feeling the most stress, to hands-on help
them achieve their goals.

But when I do this, I can't get too close. Because of lesson
number two: this year, I know, more than anyone, that you
cannot be friends with those you work with. I won't go into
details, but I've learned. It's like having that affair and saying you won't develop feelings. But then you do, things get
complicated, and you forget that it's a business you're running.
You can go to happy hour with your teammates. You can have
lunch with them. You can celebrate. You can joke. But I've
learned that you can't get too close. You shouldn't gab with
them about personal relationships. You probably shouldn't invite them to that housewarming party. Don't hang out with
them on the weekends. There's a narrow but notable difference in work friendships and "real-world" friendships. Respect
that line. Enough said.

So, I may not be the queen bee expert on hiring, and I'm
happy(er) to say that now. I can say that now. But I do have
people in my circle who are badasses at crafting teams, and I
bow down to them. Hiring matters. And despite what a lot of
first-time founders may think, it matters the most at the very
beginning. When you're tiny, every little heartbeat on the team
counts for something. Every person you add can help you soar
or completely rock the boat (or sink it altogether). Team dynamics are the most fragile when you're scrappy; energy rubs
off like static electricity, moving constantly from one individual
to the next. In these earliest stages, you're operating not just a

business but a teeter-totter, and balancing it takes a hell of a lot more than luck.

So, you're going to want to hire fast. But strive to do so thoughtfully. Think hard about the values you need on your team, the resources you need, how much time you truly require. Trust your gut feeling but get others to interview newbies as well to double-check your assessments.

When I'm hiring someone new for Girls in Tech, I ask myself these questions:

- What do I want this hire to accomplish? I try to fixate not on the job title but rather on what I want to get done every day. What should this person be doing that will make me happy and make a difference in the organization? For example, you may think you need a PR person at first because you need a press release written. But perhaps you just need a content manager instead. Or you may want to update your web pages, but you can do it with an SEO professional rather than a web developer. Thinking about the specific outcomes you're looking for will help guide you to the right professional.

- Where are the current barriers and skills gaps? Is there something that you need that you might be missing? It's a good idea to ask your current team members about where they see skills gaps and barriers.

- Where do they need to be physically located? Does it matter if they reside in San Francisco?

- How many hours a week will this person be working? Do I have enough work for this person to fill forty hours of his or her time?

- How does this person prefer to work and collaborate? Some people love a phone call, others pretend their phone isn't getting service. Your styles should match.

- If it's a remote worker, how do they structure their days, and what can we at Girls in Tech expect as far as communication and frequency of check-ins?

- Who will this person be working with most, internally or externally? What do those people expect in interactions and experience levels? For example, Girls in Tech's executive partners expect a far more polished experience than our events vendors might.

- How does this person like to receive feedback?

- Why Girls in Tech and why now? What interests this person about our organization beyond needing a paycheck?

One area in particular to chew on: consider whether you need someone freelance or full time. This doesn't seem like a tough question, but it can be. Many start-up founders turn to freelance contractors to fill holes, as they should. It's an affordable, easy way to scale up or down as you need without the burden of long-term commitment.

However, if you do go the freelance route, remember, they aren't on your team full time. So that means you cannot hold full-time expectations over them. You can't expect them to answer to every demand, every whim. Heck, you can't even necessarily expect them to be free to do that rush project you thought about at 11 last night. They don't owe you a schedule or an explanation of where they are on any given day, what they're up to, or what other projects fill their plate. If you're looking to bring on a few freelancers, ask yourself whether you need them full time (as in, butts in the seat at your start-up garage) or a few hours a week, and ask them what level of commitment they can offer you. Get super-clear, up front, about time lines and expectations about turnaround times. And consider process: How will this person submit work or gather approvals? Who on your team do you need your new employee to link up with so that you, as the founder and CEO, aren't getting overly buried?

Working through this list will help you think through how this person may fit in or affect your culture.

I rattle off this list with ease—but remember, I'm still learning. I've gotten better in this past decade, but I'm not there yet. Sometimes I need to choke out this admission, but knowing your weaknesses is one of the biggest hurdles of being a founder.

✳

Because I'm not there yet, I spoke to some incredible women who are. Alvina Antar, for example. Alvina serves as the CIO for Zuora. She's been a relentless supporter of Girls in Tech for several years. She's the woman who always shows up. Who beams with pure pride. (And she gives amazing hugs!) Before Zuora, Alvina was at Dell, where she had all the bells and whistles a giant enterprise could afford her—big team, big resources, that kind of thing. She left a few years ago to head to Zuora, a late-stage tech start-up, to head up their technology team.

Alvina told me about the natural tipping point many companies reach, where they realize they need more infrastructure and standards in place to scale. She offers a fresh perspective on what it's like to go from global enterprise to start-up mode. She also shared what she is looking for when she evaluates new candidates—and why allowing people to truly own their role is critical.

In the earliest days of a start-up, tech can function as a bit of a collage. Scratch that. *Everything* can be a collage . . . it's like navigating a giant jungle where you can only see so far in front of you. You just do the best you can. It may be up to a bunch of engineers and miscellaneous freelancers to achieve the initial vision for the company, a vision that may be constantly changing to better address product-market fit and investor feedback. Each team member is expected to multitask, and sometimes an overarching strategy can get left behind in all the craze.

But here's where Alvina says this can go wrong: "When you talk about start-ups, everything is happening a hundred miles an hour. Investments are being made by different leaders in a company, whether it's sales or finance or engineering, and it's all being done in vacuums because no one has time to talk . . . .There's not any one person who is accountable for the end-to-end ecosystem of the business, until you invest in a CIO."

This is an example of the cleanup process that often occurs at start-ups when teams are stuck in the moment. Teams can get stuck on the "problem right now" rather than thinking about long-term needs and planning for growth. Everyone is moving fast and trying to accomplish their tasks, but that may mean Band-Aid fixes, multiple versions of collaboration software, confusion about technology investments. Thinking more carefully up front about who you need on your team in the early days can help to avoid these challenges.

In this instance, when a true CIO is eventually hired, the challenge is that companies then must do a bit of cleanup, some backpedaling. They've been sailing for a while and things are going "okay," but in order to scale they now need to work toward *flawless* instead. A technology cleanup ensues, something that can be incredibly costly and time consuming.

To avoid this, Alvina noted, consider hiring a strategic role like a CIO on the early side. "Companies wait until this tipping point where they realize they have way too many duplicate capabilities. There aren't really standards. The systems aren't integrated. The processes are all manual. And so, the company is not efficient. And with manual processing comes errors and compliance issues. How do you pre-empt that? I want to get to the point where this [CIO] role is something you invest in early on, make the right decisions so you're not in cleanup mode."

The same could be said for many roles at a start-up. Therefore, it's crucial to think not only about roles but about long-term outcomes you want each hire to work toward. Roles affect outcomes, period. Consider data, for example. Who manages data and analytics at an early stage start-up to ensure they're being captured, stored, and accessed in the best way possible? This could be the founder, it could be marketing, or it could be an engineer. Regardless, if this isn't handled properly, not only will there be a cleanup to look forward to in a few years but also a potentially devastating loss of customer information.

I don't want to overwhelm you. Figuring out who to hire when you're just a few years in is not an easy call. Most of you are just trying to get your idea off the ground, and you only daydream of the challenge of mapping out a broader team. It's all about balance. In the earliest days of a start-up, you probably won't have a massive tech infrastructure or tons of e-mail data, but someone on the team (Who will it be? You need to decide.) still needs to think about long-term strategy. This may mean hiring various consultants or freelancers to evaluate your setup with fresh eyes and to advise you on these matters. It may seem silly, but setting yourself up on the front end for success with the right structure, team, and tools in place will save you time and money later. It'll be mostly time that you care about. Once you start selling to customers and gaining traction, you're going to have your eyes on growth. It will be even harder to tear away and to go back and "fix" these early-stage fundamentals.

But it was this challenge for Alvina that made the role at Zuora so appealing. Alvina was attracted to a late-stage start-up versus a super-duper early stage because she knew that a company like

Zuora would be willing to make the *investment* in a CIO. That's
what it is, an investment in hiring the right people. They were
ready for it. She assumed that, by then, they understood what
they were working toward and held some appreciation for what
a CIO could do for them. Now, it's Alvina's responsibility to
make sure Zuora is making the right technology investments,
signing the right contracts, tracking analytics to measure long-
term impact. She's creating standards and processes that will
enable the organization to take off. Worth every dime.

And, of course, a huge part of Alvina's responsibilities is
building out her team. To do so, she trusts her gut more than
anything, but she also looks for someone who sets the bar high
for success: "Whoever you are hiring, technology is changing.
You must know that the person has foundational, deep knowledge and hunger to be able to stay current, to not just learn
things to be able to do the job. You can't teach standards of
excellence. The individual has to have an inherent drive. Status
quo is not acceptable. Mediocracy is not acceptable."

These folks will come into a culture of true intrapreneurship. The culture at Zuora revolves around the concept of being
your own boss, your own CEO.

"Everyone should be empowered to make decisions as if
this were your own company, as if you were running the ship.
We don't hire individual contributors that we want to say, 'I
made this decision because so-and-so told me to do it.' That's
BS. We should do what we feel is right, as if it were our own
company."

Are you listening, founders? You're going to have to un-
clench your grip on the micro aspects of your company as you
build your team. Let people make their own decisions and take
ideas and run with them. We discussed this in the intrapreneurship chapter, too—but if you can't trust your team to run
with something, then you're in the wrong job. Effective leaders
encourage independence, decision making, innovative ideas. If

you're the micromanaging type, then you might as well fold your cards now.

"For start-up founders, it's so important to have a culture that respects individual thought and individual decisions. Talk about innovation. How can you innovate—by creating an innovation team on the side?" Alvina asked. "That's BS. The only way you innovate is to make everyone *feel* they can innovate."

And this is why HR departments and management classes the world over talk about cross-functional development. It's a way for people to break out of their cookie-cutter roles to collaborate and truly innovate. It's a way to foster creativity and create new opportunities for team members to learn and grow.

The best part? It doesn't take budget to not be an asshole. Hire the best people you can and then let them rock your start-up.

"If you have a team of people who are just order takers, who are just waiting for the next ask, that's not a recipe for success."

❋

Alyson Welch is another leadership ninja, but in the sales department. Start-ups get the ball rolling with engineering, but, once they've reached a viable product, they lean almost entirely on sales and marketing to hit the pavement and get the word out. Think of your sales team as your soldiers in the field; they are hugely important to your survival. Creating and building long-standing relationships with clients and prospects will make or break your success, almost more than your core product (yes, relationships are everything!).

Finding those first customers is mission-critical to your long-term success. Start-ups need to be willing to shape the product to these first customers. Build for them. Solve their pain points. Listen to what they say. Follow their user experience. Be ready and willing to pivot and to mold your business to meet their needs.

These early customers have an opportunity, as do you. They can become your greatest advocates and brand ambassadors. It may not be their start-up, but they're going to play a huge part in molding your direction and deciding upon your course. For some of you, this may be a tough thing to swallow—the whole idea that you don't always know what's right—but if you can go with it and listen, you'll be setting yourself up for massive success.

Here's the deal with Alyson. Her background at one point almost entirely focused on *enterprise, enterprise, enterprise*. Big bucks, bigger business, and a crapload of resources were at her disposal to turn sales calls into mega-contracts. Notably, she was with Akamai, with a national responsibility, driving approximately 10 percent of its sales revenue, a big deal for a $2 billion tech company.

She decided to change gears and took her enterprise expertise to Start-up Land, where she was the first head of sales for a pre-revenue start-up based in San Francisco that specialized in media intelligence. She described it as a "rapid communications platform"—a way for companies to carve their narrative and strategically leverage storytelling. She was excited to make the move, to do something different, to apply her enterprise polish to a scrappy start-up environment.

However, she admitted that she was a bit taken aback by the drastic differences in the two worlds. She was surprised by many of the resources that she had counted on heavily in the enterprise world, things that just didn't exist in her new one.

"I knew it was going to be my third child and that I'd be building this with heart and soul and commitment. But some things that I took for granted in the big corporate environment were the communication patterns, the schedule, the infrastructure." She notes that even things like, "does the phone work?"—well, she couldn't count on it. Or scheduling meetings and administrative support—well, there was no obvious resource or ownership of those tasks. The same thing goes for tracking sales calls and monitoring important statistics, because at the start-up everyone just dialed straight from their cell phones.

Her biggest challenge, however, was the hiring. The board was eager to hire and scale, to hit the market hard. By this time, the company had achieved some success through evangelist selling techniques, and now it was time to get serious and hire an army. Yet, like with many start-ups, there were strict limits on compensation. It wasn't as though Alyson could just hire her dream team and call it a day. She found herself limited to a midrange of experience. In parallel, she herself had to learn the product, refine the pitch, and understand what the lead-to-conversion process really looked like.

She was immediately hit with the reality that the talent pool for her budget wasn't smack-in-the-face impressive.

What I found was disappointing in the market in that range . . . Salesforce, Oracle, IBM, Adobe. A lot of the tech companies that have grown in the last ten to fifteen years have built these amazing lead machines that feed the sales-people prospects and opportunities. The traditional profile of a salesperson who has five to eight years [of experience] has come into an environment where marketing is some-what already established. There is already a marketing en-gine putting the brand out there, talking about the product, warming up the phones. So, when the sales rep gets involved, the skids are already greased.

Not so in the start-up world. No one knew who they were. There was zilch brand recognition. And the reps that came through the door weren't necessarily used to having to do the cold call thing. "Because I had been in this larger company environment for so long, I wasn't acclimated to the importance of warming up the market," she said.

Looking back, she understands that, in a start-up environment, warming up the market through marketing and understanding a lead strategy is critical—something that should probably be accomplished before you bring on a team of sales reps (with no leads to send their way). A start-up should understand what its brand value is, how it is perceived, the barriers to entry, who it is targeting specifically. These nuts and bolts are areas where any start-up should slow down and map out before bringing on clients. Additionally, a start-up needs to map out pricing (Are there different levels? Is pricing based on ad hoc features?), the training element (How can start-ups help their new clients train their in-house teams? What resources will be made available?) and, of course, service (What happens when something goes wrong? How do clients request help or report bugs?).

Start-ups must remember that not everyone who is a good schmoozer makes a good salesperson. It takes more than that to survive in a cutthroat market.

"You have to be intellectually curious, especially in a start-up," Alyson suggested. "[You must possess] an interest or fascination with solving problems for your customers. You're not just punching in or punching out, you're really trying to bring something that is transformative to the business."

✳

Psssst. I have to tell you, hiring is just *one part* of the overall team engine.

People problems are something many start-up founders struggle with. People problems can and will destroy you. From what I've observed, this challenge often completely sideswipes founders. They can be so head-in-the-sand when it comes to this—they're up close and personal with their start-up. They're all about control. They're optimists and they go to bed dreaming about all the possibilities. So, when they have an issue with someone on their team, there's often a reaction like, "Holy shit, where did this *come from?*"

I'm talking about infighting. Clarifications of roles and re-sponsibilities. Power struggles with your founding members. Confusion over company vision. Budget disputes. People hav-ing different priorities. These issues will slowly eat away at the heart of your start-up. Bringing someone on your team is just one step in the team-management process. It's not a check-box item. It's the beginning of what you should hope to be a long journey. You may be obsessed with your product development or knee-deep in technical issues, but you can't zone out of lead-ing the team.

Once you bring someone on your team—even a remarkable person who takes initiative and can really run the show (Yay, an intrapreneur at heart!)—you still need to be a freakin' leader. Your team will still look to you to set a strategic direction for your company, to check in with them, to make fast decisions. You can't hire and then tune out with a Corona. You've got to be on it. *All the time.* I'm not talking about not trusting your team and micromanaging. I'm talking about being present and willing to guide your start-up. A lot of twentysomething found-ers and start-up leaders haven't really considered this part of entrepreneurship until they're knee-deep in it and are expe-riencing issues. People who are unhappy. People quitting (Say what? They don't believe in your mission?).

I'll admit, managing the team has taken me aback. It takes a LOT of time, and, remember, I'm leading an organization that only has a few folks (fewer than ten, people!) compared to later-stage start-ups. I've noticed it's a two-way thing: My em-ployees look to me to check in, to meet with them, to guide them. But at the same time, I fight my inner urge to constantly micromanage and have a say in every little detail. You can't have both and still be effective. You need to know when to step back and when to dig your hands deep in the mud.

Here's a few ways I've managed to conquer some people-related woes. For one, I call myself out on my inner paranoia. You know, the voice in my head that wants to dictate it all and spout off, Rainman-style. *Whoa, slow down, Adriana.* When I find myself getting the urge to micromanage or being emotionally reactive to whatever, I often will just take twenty-four hours to decompress and let things marinate. Then, when I re-approach the situation, I can do so with a fresh mind.

Second, I have gone out of my way to hire in a much more thoughtful manner. That means I don't just hire the first person I like, but I give my team time to evaluate, and I lean heavily on my board to do the same. I collect feedback from multiple individuals to paint a story of a candidate. Does this slow the process down? You betcha. Has it saved me days, weeks, months on the back end by hiring people who are a better fit? Yes! And that's why it's all worth it.

Third, I've learned that one of the easiest ways to make for happy employees is to just show up. Show up for meetings. Respect their time. Make one-on-one meetings a top priority. Just show up and listen. It's the most low-hanging fruit of all ways to respect people you work with.

And, finally, along the time theme, I never, ever ask employees to work evenings or weekends. Never. I cherish my weekends as part of my striving for something that resembles balance, whatever that is. And I have to do the same for the people I work with. So, I don't get fixated on hours in the office, on clocking in and clocking out, and so on. It's not about where you're seated or the hours but the output. And I want people on my team who are rested and know that they can take time to breathe when they need to. Because I've been there. This isn't to say that we don't work our asses off; it's just a reality check on priorities and how things get executed.

WHAT DID WE LEARN?

✓ **Be prepared. Building a team is rough.**

It seems sexy. You're in charge! You might have some seed moolah to spend! You get to be a CEO! But before you slap on those shades and stroll down Sandhill Road, remember: what you really are is chief recruiter and evangelist. You need to first convince people to work for you. You need to find talent, which will be a balance between managing your extremely limited budget and finding people you can count on. If you're doing it with pure sweat equity alone, you're in a crap position—you need to hand over a lot of equity to make the offer worthwhile, and you need to work even harder to find that perfect fit.

Always be thinking about your talent bench. Don't wait until you need to fill a role to look for that perfect person; you need to be a 24/7 talent scout. This means networking, planning, and working your every connection.

✓ **Don't just hire for skill. Hire for leadership.**

The allure of a power trip is real, but resist it with everything you've got. The last thing you need is to hire people who can't take initiative. You want a team who is smarter than you. You want a team who will confidently make decisions and not have to ask you every *Goddamn day* whether they are doing things right. So, step back and let them do their shiny thing. Trust them—even if it fights against every cell in your body and you've got a burning ringworm urge to micromanage the F out of 'em.

√ **Managing a team will be a time suck.**

Plan for it. Then plan for it even more, and carve out even more time than you originally anticipate. Get your head in a place where you are mentally prepared to be pulled in many directions; get ready to flex an entirely new part of your brain: part therapist, part manager, part hands-on ninja. You'll still need to get in the weeds, but, at the same time, you'll also be looked to for inspiration and motivation, to create a cohesive vision for your team. You'll either naturally sail through this, or you'll tread in the water until pure exhaustion hits. It's okay to not get it right the first time (or the tenth—remember, I'm right there with ya on the learning carousel).

CHAPTER 9

Innovation

SO, WHAT ARE you going to do now with all the resources at your disposal? Make magic happen? Disrupt? Innovate? And what the heck does that even mean, really?

Innovation is an elusive, ambiguous concept. At a glance, it's a word that people in tech circles throw around often; it's one of those overused, annoying business words that have the power to make you cough up your morning coffee and gluten-free bagel. *Innovation. Scale. Optics. Synergy. Next generation.*

It's like many companies think that calling themselves innovative or calling their creations "innovation" simply makes it so. Innovation is something that I think everyone is searching for, but it's not something you can just define—you'll know it when you get there. It's not a label, it's a place.

Airbnb is innovative. It's taken this old-school notion of hotels—as though that's all you have available to you when you travel—and completely shattered it. Airbnb has shifted an entire industry on its head, and it's convinced consumers and homeowners alike to think differently about how we share and interact with each other.

And Uber—for all its failings from a culture perspective and despite all the ways it's let us down—is innovative. No one can deny it. In thousands of people's minds, Uber has replaced taxis—entirely. Uber has completely switched out its service for a service that thrived for decades and decades, for something that you probably, just five or ten years ago, never thought would fall out of existence. That very concept, that an entire service can be here one day and then gone the next, is utterly fascinating to me. Here one day, gone the next.

Raise your hand if you still pay for cable. Raise your hand if you can't even remember what cable is or why you even bothered. Thanks to the likes of Netflix, many of us find better programming, far more entertaining and edge-of-our-seat quality, than the generic stuff that plays across the FCC-controlled cable airways. And, remember, Netflix didn't just change the delivery of programs, it took the bull by the horns and became a premium content creator. I remember its first iteration, the little envelopes of DVDs in the mail. At the time, that was pure awesome: the idea of never going to a brick-and-mortar Blockbuster store again to browse on a dead Friday night, to receive it right to your mailbox. The ease and convenience, the effortlessness of it. And that wasn't too many years ago. When Netflix went completely online, that blew a lot of people's minds. *Wait, I can receive content now? This very minute? In a freakin' click?* The very definition of on demand. You want it, you ask for it, you get it—NOW.

And just look at today's children! They grow up and become toddlers and stumble toward their televisions like miniature drunks. They're not just coming in for an image close-up. Rather, they try to swipe the TV with their little paws, like they're working a seventy-five-inch iPad. I've seen friends' toddlers swipe smartphones with the ease and nonchalance of a Google software developer. And they can open up, browse, and save their favorite Amazon Prime shows to Mommy and Daddy's account with disturbing familiarity. For better or worse, this is their world—one run by pixels and connections and batteries and cloud-enabled apps. And it makes the one I grew up in look startlingly antiquated.

It's progress. This is what progress looks like.

It's what all high-growth start-ups on the planet aim for, what they dream about when they think about coming to market. This is what venture capitalists dream about too. They're looking for the next Airbnb, the next Uber, the next Facebook. They're looking for world-changing, mind-altering technologies that don't just enhance our lives but drastically change the way we live, that become ingrained in our culture and the way we conquer our every day. For VCs and founders, this is a gamble— a pricy gamble—worth making bets on. Isn't this the kind of success you're aiming for? Tell me, reader, that you don't go to bed at night thinking about changing the world on this level, completely revolutionizing the way we live our lives. Most of you aren't doing this just to make money. You're reaching for the stars and pushing the limits of what's possible. You're testing the limits of yourself, of technology, and of society. You want to be the woman who dreamed up an entire new way of living, which requires groundbreaking innovation.

WHAT INNOVATION TAKES

Enter Hilary Weber, founder and CEO of Opportu Startup Innovation. Hilary is much more than a coach, though coaching is one thing she does for start-up leaders. What she really does is partner with start-ups and other organizations to help fine-tune their team development, the way they interact with each other, the way they approach product development, how they approach problem solving. She deconstructs the inner dialogues of an organization; she facilitates effective, productive interactions; she pushes start-ups to the edge of their comfort zone to get them to think differently about how they work. Girls in Tech has been lucky to have partnered with Hilary on numerous occasions to facilitate curriculum and workshops for our global member base.

Innovation kicks off with an idea. But you're probably wondering how to know whether it's going to be worth your while. How do you know whether it's big enough to dedicate your everything to—your life, your bank account, your mental and physical energy? Hilary said it's all about the customer response. You don't have innovation until you're fulfilling a real customer need.

"You are not going to know for sure until you can validate it with your potential customers. As Steve Blank says, 'Get out of the building!' (In other words, go talk with people and find out what they really need)," Hilary explained. "That's the entire reason for creating an MVP (minimum viable product) instead of a perfect, polished one. Too often I see founders fall in love with their idea, and they are so sure that it will be a hit that they either don't test it hard enough or ignore the signs that there really isn't a solid market for what they are building."

This is the classic case of operating in a wind tunnel. I've made the mistake of doing this myself from time to time. For example, there are several times I've been overly confident in programming for Girls in Tech members. I just knew—in my core—that a boot camp was needed or that we needed to open a chapter in a certain location. But not getting out of the building, to use Steve Blank's description, is an early landmine many founders can stumble right into. Companies of all sizes encounter this issue, it's definitely not limited to Start-up Land. But it's a reminder that asking your customers what they need can help solve your woes. Customers hold the clues. They will guide you more than you can imagine if you just let them.

Hilary warned that another stumbling block for founders involves change (Eek! That terrifying word again!). Founders can get tied at the umbilical cord to an idea. They believe in it so much that they can't imagine it failing (damn optimists!). But, to let an idea flourish, you have to let it get away from you, to morph, to take shape. To get kicked around a bit and iterated upon.

"The idea will change—make no mistake," Hilary said. "What you do want to dedicate yourself to instead is the overarching vision for how the world could change in a particular area (e.g., climate change, financial services, health care, education). Having a burning passion to create change in a particular area is something I DO advocate for strongly. But hold on to your actual idea lightly, because it will wiggle, morph, and evolve over time, hopefully to arrive at a strong product-market fit."

But beware. If it's a killer idea, there's a good chance that someone else has come up with it before. Perhaps they've even put it out there to the public. Who are your competitors? What other like services or products exist? These don't need to mimic yours to a tee, but they may be like paths that consumers take to achieve the same end goal.

The point is, make sure your idea is even more killer than theirs. Know how you're going to define your business and set it apart, make it unique. Not only will customers need this information to be confident about counting on you, but this will likely be one of the first things investors ask you about.

Hilary is a proponent of small teams and fast iterating to come up with new product angles. She's a big promoter of agile processes, such as scrum meetings and working fast to come up with the aforementioned MVP. It doesn't have to be perfect or sparkly or anything too close to that; it just needs to be something that outsiders (ideally, your target customer) can play around with.

"The longer you 'polish the chrome' on your widget, the easier it will be for a competitor to motor past you and start building market share," Hilary warned. "And if you keep perfecting your product, it may be pleasing to you but not to your customers (at least not enough customers to give you a viable marketplace). You are NOT your customer—and even if you love the product, are there really millions of you? You need to find proof of that."

A great way to test your product early on is crowdfunding. Not only is this a line of seed money to help you get things going, but if you can actually raise some moolah, it's a great sign that your product is the real deal—it's actually something that people are willing to put their money toward. In essence, through crowdfunding you're compiling a database of hungry early customers.

Investors may respond well to this—and why wouldn't they? Customers are a good thing! If you can gain significant traction whatsoever, this is proof to them that you aren't full of shit. Not only are you going to them and saying, "See, I have an idea that people respond well to," but "you also have customers who are waiting to make a purchase." Pure gold.

CO-INNOVATE WITH EARLY CUSTOMERS

Another innovation strategy: build for your early customers. Build for them as though you were a custom shop and you only have, say, two to six clients. Build to their pain points, their specifications, their user experience. This is what's known as co-innovation. You create something new and pull your customers into early conversations and bring them along for the ride. This is a powerful strategy because you're able to directly connect to customers, listen to their needs, and address them in the build process. And, while you're at it, why not create a sales contract as you're going through this process? If you're really building something that they need, that they are helping you build, the smart thing to do would be to fold yourself into their budgeting cycle and get some signatures on the dotted line. Again, then you're going to VCs with real customers, a tested product, and real demand. Platinum, baby. In parallel, you're creating brand ambassadors along the way—your product's earliest cheerleaders. Invaluable.

"Another idea I heard from an entrepreneur giving a talk on sales or growth hacking was to give a talk and have everyone in the audience use [the product] in real time," Hilary said. "Bam! A hundred instant users. Rinse and repeat. The real test will be, Do they continue to use it?"

One surefire way to jumpstart a chain of customers, Hilary said, is to build in virality. No, I'm not talking about YouTube videos where a dude dances Gangnam-style (I know, you watched it too) but features within your product that naturally promote sharing. Hilary used Zoom video as an example. It's a collaboration tool, so she uses it for meetings every week. The people she meets have great experiences with it, so they get it stuck in their head. And at some point, when they're just dying to have a good video chat, they may sign up for it. The same goes for tools like Screenhero, Trello, Snap, and really anything where you collaborate and pull in other users who trust you and count you as a member of their circle. Of course, this may not work for all products, but if it works for yours, run with it and enjoy the free advertising!

And, to even out the teeter-totter, one way that is certainly NOT guaranteed to rake in more customers: money. Money is great, but it doesn't *buy you customers*. A good product-market fit gets you customers, coupled with a strong brand promise (turns out, people don't want to do business with assholes). So, if you've gotten to MVP, if you have a product ready to roll out the door, or if you have a SaaS company ready to rock—but no one is buying into it—ask yourself why. Take the time to do the digging, because throwing more budget at it may not fix things.

And, finally, realize that you need to create a company that fosters ideation and creativity, not just thinking outside the box but crushing the box. Think about start-ups; imagine a fun, nimble small business. What comes to mind? Many times, these places will have funky furniture. Orange walls. Floor-to-ceiling white boards. Friday office happy hours, where swills of vodka will emerge from co-space desks. These things are all fun, but what are they driving to, beneath the surface? These miscellaneous perks are often a company's little darts at getting their innovation engines revved up. After all, ideas spring forth when people feel comfortable sharing them. Your team needs to feel at ease with being silly, thinking outrageously, connecting with each other, and sharing information without judgment. That's a tall order.

"Many start-ups have a fun, open culture, at least in the beginning, since the team is small, there are many things to do, and things move pretty fast," Hilary said. "I feel that culture is unfortunately taken for granted in most start-ups, and that can be a fatal mistake." Hilary's point is that you need to fuel your team and glue them together through a common mission. This can serve as a foundation for making extraordinary things happen.

And as far as product development goes, if you want to make something kick-ass—that will truly rock your customers' world—then you need to sit back on your haunches, shut up, and observe. You need to see customers using your product or service. Be a fly on the wall. Watch the magic unfold and all of the bugs and crap, too. You may find that customers struggle with your product but have a hard time articulating why—what it's missing, what they don't like. So you can ask, but carve out the time to watch them too.

Take heed: not every customer is going to be an ideal first customer. It's going to be tempting to just say yes to everyone who bites (sort of like hiring can be), but think carefully. The right early customers will understand that you're in the business of inventing. The right early customers will understand that your business won't be all shiny, clean, and error-free. They'll have some level—a reasonable level—of taste for risk and reward. They're going to be looking for a service to help them do something, to change the way they operate; they won't necessarily expect unblemished perfection.

Another thing regarding early customers. Hilary warned of the other temptation, the one to just bow down to the big early customers. You may feel so ecstatic to get these folks on your side, to have them in your portfolio, that you may lean toward becoming a yes-person, with the urge to check the box and deliver upon their every whim and every request. That's wonderful from a customer service perspective—sign a sister up!—but where are you taking your company? Who is really in charge here? What's your long-term vision?

"Sometimes the hardest thing to do is say no to a big sale to stay the course toward your company goals," said Hilary.

PRODUCT DEVELOPMENT FOR THE WIN

To get more good stuff on product development, I spoke with Donna Boyer, former director of product for Airbnb and now VP of product for Stitch Fix. Impressive credentials, no? Yeah, she knows her thing when it comes to product. And she's candid that product is one of those funky niche focus areas. Product folks drive so much of strategy, they are accountable for the shape of a product and the user experience, yet they typically don't have charge of the team (developers, designers, and the like) who actually executes their vision. And, as she says, you either love it or it drives you crazy; she falls into the love camp. Big time.

Start-ups may not hire a product person right out the gate, but it's not unusual for product managers to be in the bunch of early hires. There's too much to watch, too much to catch, too much happening, and all too fast to let it slide. Once your start-up has some sort of footing, a product manager can be the person you pass the ball to. He or she is not driving the strategy for your company but is the person you can count on to become obsessive about your users, the data behind their actions, the minutiae of details that can make the difference between a polished experience and a clunky one. A product manager is an investment worth making.

"The biggest predictor of success [in product development] is just straight-up critical thinking skills," Donna said. "You can find that in any discipline. . . . I tend to look for people who have semi-technical backgrounds because you need to be able to work closely with engineering. But it really is a blend of art and science. Just having intuition and being able to back that intuition up with metrics and data is fundamental to the job."

But Donna warned that the balance between analytics and intuition is critical. Yes, you have to look at data; you have to look at it constantly. But she said you also must have a point of view (which can often be something of a leap of faith). You have to know what you're working toward, but you can't operate without the data. So that means having a plan, formalizing a hypothesis, and being rigorous about how you measure your progress and changes.

Bring forth the inner skeptic. Question everything. Never stop asking why. Donna said she is always reminding her team to look for reasons they are wrong—not why they are right. The goal isn't to validate being on track; that doesn't do anything for you other than give you a mental pat on the back. Being right doesn't make for a good or improved product. Good product managers need to look for what they're missing, what they've missed, open their eyes to what they aren't seeing. In other words, they need to give their ego a kick to the curb. It's not about winning points, it's about doing the best thing for the customer, for the product, and for the company. Finding out where you're wrong—that's where you'll know how to grow and what to build next.

Like Hilary, Donna advocates for constant testing, as early as possible. It's the only way to be sure about your path forward. "Get your product over to real people as early as you can. And real people don't mean your friends in Silicon Valley." She laughed. "It's just that it's a very small world here."

What Donna is saying is that you need to break out of your bubble. You want to be deliberate about your testing strategy and get in front of a variety of demographics, ages, ethnicities. Work hard to gather a diversity of opinions. This is a product person's way of gathering code, DNA about users.

And it's always better to have something than nothing. So, gather data even if it's rough around the edges. Donna believes prototypes are an absolute must. You build. You test. You build. You test again. Over and over as you refine and shape your product. When we spoke, her team was working on an app for Airbnb. To put things in perspective, they were testing weekly— in front of real people. "It made all the difference in the world," she said. "You can think through on paper, but until you get hands on it, it's not good feedback. There are unpredictable ways people get confused."

You must see it to believe it. You can't be successful without testing. You can't test without interacting with customers and gathering data. You can't look at a spreadsheet full of numbers without checking your gut on what is or isn't working. Innovation is a complex web of meeting customer needs and at the same time giving customers what they didn't even know they were missing. Part process, part gut, part data.

Can't afford to spend the cash to prototype for real? You can still rough-sketch your product on paper and have people fake play with it to give you some direction so you're not wandering in the dark.

When you're making product decisions, Donna pointed out, it's really about priorities. You're setting priorities for the company and for resources, and you're playing chief navigator.

That's the heart of product; it's making the right choices. You will always have more to do than you can possibly do. You're constantly making smart tradeoffs. The only way to make those right tradeoffs is to really understand what problem you're trying to solve and why you think what you're doing is solving the problem. It's not about the what, it's about the why. Why does your choice matter and to whom does it matter?

Innovation is an idea taking flight. If you can't connect the dots between idea, customer, and data, then you're just another person with an idea. And that's not innovation.

WHAT DID WE LEARN?

✓ **Innovation starts on the inside.**
Like all aspects of a start-up, innovation needs to spark within the founder first and foremost. And then you need to cascade it to your team. Everything begins at the top—innovation, values, respect. Founders can innovate the crap out of their product, but no one succeeds on their own. So, you need to give your team the tools (*ahem*, the culture) to innovate on its own. This means letting go of any fantasy of being a perfectionist, giving your team the room to breathe (and to fail!). It can also mean "cute" things like giving team members creative outlets—you know, adorable little plants on their desks, the classic foosball experience, and a fresh pack of whiteboard markers.

But it's more than that. It's encouraging them to think on their own and rewarding ideas and radical new concepts. You're going to be under pressure to move fast, and that's normal. You can't snail your way to the top, but you can carve out time in your days and weeks to share ideas, question your mode of attack, and try to look through a different lens.

✓ Cater to early customers, but maintain control.

We all want to say yes to the people who help us. For start-ups, it's those very first customers. For me, it can be bigwig corporate sponsors, the ones my organization relies on to breathe. We can all feel a bit of the "yes reflex" kicking in sometimes. You want to say yes to those you need. You want to say yes to those who have been good to you. I know this more than anyone—I'm saying yes all the time, and then, frankly, I lose sleep at night wondering whether I can really pull things off. (*Note to self: just stop that!*)

I can imagine the deep appreciation for your earliest customers, the ones who walk away from stable enterprises to gamble on you. There's such a thrill in the idea of building something together, of embarking on a new product journey—together. But, at the same time, you still need to be at the helm of the ship. If you're in the construction industry, and your customers want you to make software for custom makeup palettes, maybe it's not a good fit. There's only so far you can go off course without turning in circles.

✓ Gather hands-on data or bust!

If you haven't gotten this point now, go back at least five pages and reread. Get the message tattooed on your forehead: don't make a product without seeing what customers think. The key word here is "seeing": see what they think—

you can't rely on them to tell you. For example, they may hate your design, but maybe they're clicking all the right buttons and navigating through your app like a click mae-stro. That's a good thing. Maybe they say they just "don't like it," but you can see, from your hours of testing and obser-vation, that they're getting frustrated from the start at your shitty login page.

Go on, grasshopper. Watch your customers in their natu-ral habitat. And learn.

✓ Question everything.

Data, data, data. Sometimes we can be so into it, so head-deep, in spreadsheets that we miss the big picture. Data is crucial to product development and innovating with a mis-sion, but remember to balance out your numbers with your brand, your product goals, and your gut. Bringing both sides of the story together will give you a more complete picture of what's going on, where the problems lie, and what you may need to change.

Become your own most annoying skeptic. Don't let your-self fall victim to comfort. Be your company's resident de-tective, and always ask why, what you're missing, and what you're overlooking. Confidence is a good thing. But ego is the ultimate destroyer.

CHAPTER 10

Confidence

YOU MAY BE thinking, "Whoa, girl, slow down! A whole chapter on confidence?" And to that, I say, "Hell, yes!" (*Psssst, I told you so, didn't I?*) Indeed, confidence is a start-up essential. In fact, confidence is the secret weapon of any good entrepreneur. It's how we slither our way into earning the trust of new clients, how we close deals, how we lead the team (even when it may be our first time doing all these things). Confidence gets us in the door to VC meetings. It wins pitch competitions. It recruits and hires the right people to join our little growing army. In other words, confidence *sells*. It can sell just about anything.

Don't believe me? Take a few minutes and imagine a business meeting. It's led by a female founder, and she's meeting with three men. They're all white. They're all at least ten years older than she is. She's a first-time founder, whereas these guys have been around the block. They wait for her in a generic conference room—neutral colors, a glossy long table, just the whiz of the AC going to pass the time.

She arrives. She looks nervous; her face is a billboard for "Worry". She's thinks she's late, and she apologizes one time too many. The wrinkles on her forehead show a face that is used to looking concerned. Her shoulders are rolled forward, her physical way of closing off the outside world.

She doesn't smile when they greet her.

She's unsure of herself when they ask her questions.

Her handshake just sucks. It's one of those limp fish handshakes, the kind that'll give anyone the willies.

Okay now. Do you think these guys want to ever see her again? My instincts overwhelmingly say, "Ain't got time for that." If your alarm bells aren't ringing on this one, too, then you might as well throw this book to the flames now and revisit the romance with your day job.

Look, I realize what she's up against. I've been there. It's not easy walking into that cold meeting room. To have all eyes on you, expecting you to deliver something wonderful. To have to tell your pitch story to a room of nonbelievers. To feel like your heart is beating so loud they can hear it. To look into their eyes as you present and to know that they can be the bridge to life-changing capital, the money you need to see your start-up soar.

But, because it's not easy and frankly, not equitable— because these guys hold the keys to the bank—it's even more important to put your most confident self forward. Someday, the system will be more in the favor of all of us and not just a select, privileged few. In the meantime, those funders need to see that you can take it. They need to believe that you have the ability and charisma to sell your start-up when you need to find your first customers. They're not in the business of writing multimillion-dollar checks to people who stumble awkwardly through pitch meetings. They want to back the next generation of leaders, not some shy girl who can't sell her idea.

Confidence is crucial even if you're faking it. It doesn't matter if you feel like hiding as long as you keep those feelings on the inside. Think about what confidence communicates to the outside world. (Don't think about whether it's true, just think about what confidence says and does.) It tells people that you know what you're doing. It tells people that you're prepared. It says that you know your shit. It implies you're an expert.

Speaking of which—I'm not an expert in confidence. I was a shy kid, all the way to college. The kind of kid who used to hide behind Mom's legs, never ask twice, the whole don't-speak-until-you're-spoken-to sort of thing. I'm not sure why, but I do know my parents put a bit of a protective layer around me, especially in the middle school and high school years. I didn't attend a lot of parties or social functions. My curfew was em-barrassingly early: in high school, I was expected home at 9:30. Prom came and went, and, well, let's just say my dress stayed on. I stuck to the rules, I met conventional expectations. For an entrepreneur with my entrepreneurial family, I was surprisingly risk averse in my youth. This sheltered life didn't exactly help me feel like I could conquer the world. Breaking rules takes confidence, and, up through high school, I hadn't yet flirted with that idea.

I came into my own after a summer abroad. That was my high school graduation gift. Despite their protective nature, my parents knew I needed to see the world. So, at just seventeen, I was off to Europe with a friend to backpack for weeks on end. Stumbling my way through conversations in foreign languages, getting lost on cobblestone streets, and being on my own helped me emerge into a human who much more closely resembles the person I am today.

But. Doubt still creeps in. It's in this way that confidence isn't natural; it's earned, it's faked, it's shaped over a lifetime.

Just six months ago, I woke up in the quiet morning light of my Oakland apartment. I didn't rise peacefully; I felt my heart beating from the start. I sat up fast, with the alertness of some-one who never really slept well in the first place.

And I knew why: that afternoon, I had a meeting with the head of one of the top beauty brands in the United States.

This meeting loomed before me, both taunting and threatening. It was with the CEO and her closest counterparts, but this was no start-up CEO with a five-person team. This was a CEO of an established enterprise. A mature woman. A wise woman. Someone with polished leadership skills, an opinion that could cut like a knife, and a primal instinct for opportunity.

She was arriving with two other women from her crew, and she was meeting me and my core team at our San Francisco office. A major partnership deal was on the table; if I could make this thing work, it could mean big things for the organization. Yet, somewhere in the back of my mind, I had been second-guessing myself on this for weeks, months. Doubt creeped in, making me suddenly feel unsure and shaky. Everything felt, all at once, inadequate. From our silly marketing proposal to the snacks we had planned for the conversation. (Yeah, I know, of all things, I'm analyzing carrots versus cheese. But every decision felt only half right.)

I needed some confidence ammo. I bolted to my closet and pushed aside the crammed blouses and dresses and skirts. I was in search of one dress in particular: a bright red dress. Bold. Unconventional. *On fire*. The kind of dress that demands a crowd to look twice. The kind of dress that most women wouldn't wear to work.

It was just the dress I needed to look the part of a confident CEO.

And it worked. I pulled that thing on with the nonchalance of a twenty-five-year-old. I looked put together but in that enviously effortless way that so many women want to achieve, and I knew it. And I wasn't ashamed of that—rather, I embraced it. I owned it. And, that day, I put it to work for me.

Here's how I feel when I wear red: like I'm a walking billboard with a challenge. *I dare you to say no.* I'm fresh. Unabashedly in charge. Confidence oozes from my every pore. I know who I am in red, with all my faults and all my strengths, and I feel at home with each one. Red means not explaining myself. It means not saying sorry. It means not backtracking. No second guesses. It's my power color, and it's gotten me through many meetings and through countless presentations. It's been the little secret that I've leaned on throughout the years to give me a boost when I need one.

※

Let's face it. Confidence is a big deal. It's probably why psychologist Amy Cuddy's TED talk on confidence—and the magic of using power poses to build your confidence—is so widely viewed. In her talk, Amy tells how the power of physical poses can relay themselves to your psyche. The whole thing is fascinating. I believe in it because I see the difference it makes to stand tall, to raise my arms up over my head victoriously. Your physical self is a manifestation of what you feel on the inside. People always say that it's what's on the inside that counts, but I'd argue that what's on the outside matters more than many would like to admit.

Stand tall, shoulders back, and you feel confident—and those in the room with you will sense it, too. Make eye contact, and those you speak with will likely believe what you have to say. Greet people with a smile, and they're likely to want to partner with you. For me, wearing my red dress makes these simple gestures easy. It's my confidence uniform. On the outside, I'm just a sassy tech chick with a red dress. But I might as well be wearing a superhero cape.

It works, and it's free.

※

Confidence doesn't just make for a polished business meeting, it can also be the turbo-kick you need to make major life changes. No one knows this more than Marnie Rosenberg, founder of the Crossroads Coach, a consultancy where she facilitates career development coaching. Girls in Tech has worked with Marnie over the years to inspire our members, and she's also served as an incredible speaker at our annual Catalyst Conference.

Her story is interesting in that she went from a fast-paced advertising career in New York City to coaching—quite a career swing. There she was in a high-pressure industry, experiencing health challenges, caused by stress (something I'm familiar with), and she had a wake-up moment at thirty-five: nothing was going to make her situation better. That is, nothing aside from her own actions.

And so, she left without knowing what was next. She walked away, with the courage and confidence to know she'd figure it out later.

"It was totally liberating," she reflected. "In the month that followed, I didn't set my alarm clock. I meandered through my day. I started a blog. I told my world (namely, my parents) to not worry about me, and that I didn't want to talk about work for at least three months. And then, after three months, I'd be willing to think about what's next."

But there was just one thing. She noticed that she couldn't escape the dread of going back to work. She thought about what else she could do, because going back to her previous life was more frightening than anything else.

"I realized what I cared about the most was the relationships. That was the piece I cared about. What I wanted to do was work with people. . . . So, the idea of coaching came up somewhat serendipitously, and it stuck."

In her line of work, Marnie addresses lack of confidence issues regularly. She works with a range of clients. There's the entrepreneur who can't shake the negative voice in his head or who can't get rid of the inner critic about previously failed companies. Like, *It didn't work out three times before, why should it work out now? What if I can't make it work?* And the client who is thinking about leaving a job after almost two decades and is questioning, *What if it doesn't work out? I have all these things at stake.*

Marnie works with her clients to reframe their stories. She breaks down their stories and fears to pinpoint other ways to communicate the message. Her message to entrepreneurs and start-up employees: You're in charge. You tell your story. You own your story.

Marnie described reframing as this: "If you could tell that story in a different way, could you gain power from it versus feeling defeated? It's your story to tell. And you don't have to tell it as a failure."

In the case of the client who was scared to make a career transition, he couldn't shake the voice in his head that reminded him of his failures—school dropouts, delays, ghosts from the past. Yet, when he tells the story, he talks more about taking time off from school, renewing his engagement. Making a shift. Think about the change in tone when you go from "I flunked out of school" to "School was difficult for me, so I took time off and went back a little later." Same events, two different stories.

What about confronting risk aversion? Of course, entrepreneurs tend to be drawn to risk, but risk drives so much of our pressure, stress, and fear. Marnie teaches a strategy for this that she refers to as "balancing the scales." She said, with risk, your inner critic tends to gather all the evidence as to why you'll likely fail. But what if you balance the other side of the scale and gather evidence as to why you'll succeed?

"Negativity is easy. Positivity is harder," Marnie explained. "But look at where you are. You didn't get here by chance. So, if you were to own your decisions that you made to get you to this point as part of your success story, how does that make the future look? What does that change about your perspective on what is possible?"

I come back to Marnie's advice often. And this is what first-time founders need to remember. Your title or your experience or your track record doesn't matter. I'm darn sure that confidence is something we all struggle with. It's not like we rush out of the gates from college and enter the real world fearlessly. Entrepreneurs may move fast. They may embrace risk. They may seem iron clad from the outside. The same goes for VPs and CEOs at the world-class companies Girls in Tech partners with. But inside each of these women lie critics. Negative voices. Doubt.

Most of us struggle to overcome that doubt, almost daily. If you're feeling a lack of confidence, you're not alone. Work to discover what can help you overcome it, whether it's a fiery red dress, balancing the scales, or performing a slew of power poses in the bathroom before an important meeting.

✳

Sarah Bird is CEO of Moz, a well-known SEO platform for digital marketers. I'll never forget the talk she gave at Catalyst 2016. She bared her soul to the audience and told the crowd about her issues with confidence in such a refreshing, raw way. It was as though we were her buddies and she was chatting with us over stiff martinis. She told it like it is.

Her words were beyond powerful. Our blog recap of Sarah's presentation after the conference will give you an idea:

> Sarah Bird, CEO of Moz, admitted that the more responsibilities she carried and the more she rose through the ranks at Moz, the more inadequate she felt! In fact, when she was offered the position of CEO, she initially thought it a joke. The idea of negotiating her salary—asking for the compensation she deserved—formed a pit in her stomach. She was so fearful she wasn't qualified; so fearful she didn't know what she was doing.
>
> Until she said: Fuck it.

"My belief that other people know what they are doing is not true. No one does," Bird said.

She pointed out that research shows men often apply to jobs if they have about 60% of the qualifications, whereas women typically only apply if they have 100% of the qualifications. There's a major confidence gap. It's very real and it's self-limiting. "I realized I am part of the problem. No man did this to me. It was me, exploiting my own self."[1]

Sarah joined in 2007 when Moz started selling software. She was the eighth person on the tight-knit team and started off in a legal-operations role. When Sarah and I chatted, she offered myriad insights into the early days of a company. Just like onstage, she was candid with me about her stumbles through those first board meetings (she says she's still learning, even now), early hiring decisions, and simply learning the business. Frankly, I struggled with where to place Sarah in this book, because I believed she belonged in almost every chapter. But the way she navigated the unknowns and dealt with uncertainty—and still openly admits to battling these challenges—led me to putting her here, in the confidence chapter. I did this because so much of confidence is tied to knowledge and preparation and to perceived beliefs about who is or is not an expert on this or that topic.

Sarah stomps on all these notions. Rather than cower from the unknown, she seemingly embraces it. She openly admitted, onstage, during Catalyst 2016 that she didn't immediately have the confidence to own her role as CEO. In fact, when it was initially offered to her, she dismissed it. Even laughed. She thought, *why me?* She said she didn't negotiate her salary as aggressively as she should have.

At the time, she didn't have the *confidence*. And, frankly, like all of us who are new to this game, she just didn't yet know the ropes, which is not her fault. But she found her way.

For example, her first board meeting. She knew the fundamentals, especially with her background in law. They met at a
little dive restaurant in Seattle, and Sarah admitted that they
didn't have any solid materials planned in advance of that first
meeting, no financials, no strategy, nada. However, this is where
the support of her board members came through. One member took her aside and cheerfully told her that she'd be glad
to share a template for a presentation deck for a future board
meeting. Check!

"At that time, honestly, we didn't understand our own business model clearly. It was SaaS, and it was self-service SaaS, a
new kind. The quality [of the meeting] was bad because our
understanding was bad," she reflected.

To overcome the unknown Sarah does what we all do more
than we like to admit: she Googles like hell to find answers when
she runs into a wall (because why not?), and she reads a lot.

> It's so important for leaders to remain humble and keep
> learning. Don't take any leadership skill for granted. One of
> my frustrations is that we have this cultural mythology that
> leaders are born. I don't think that's true at all. My experi-
> ence is that there are skills you can learn. You can learn to
> be more self-aware. You can learn how to communicate. You
> can learn how to be a better storyteller. You can learn how
> to be a better listener. You can learn a lot of the things that
> will make you a better leader, if you keep working at them.
> The most important thing to do is to admit you're on a life-
> long journey and then invest heavily in your time.

Sarah admirably invests in her time. And I believe her; she
speaks from a place of humility. She turns to books and mentors
for answers. She takes classes and joins leadership peer groups
to open herself to new ideas. She surrounds herself with people who challenge her to gain what she refers to as "the gift of

feedback." (Because, let's face it: people don't like to criticize the boss.)

Knowledge gives you confidence. Experience gives you confidence. First-time founders may not have these tools to tap into, but take a hint from Sarah's playbook: just ask questions. Own it. Sarah's ability to ask questions and push herself to learn new things has not only shaped her ability to lead, it's given her confidence.

✳

Me? I've got a few tricks up my sleeve, beyond armoring myself with red dresses and sassy red lipstick. I also source confidence from preparation. I've learned to do this the hard way. I've fucked up a few times, big-time screw-ups, when I just haven't been prepared. When I've been moving too fast to think ahead to the next step, when I've slipped and I got careless, thinking it didn't matter as much (it did). And it's during those times that my former boss's *"No excuses!"* scolding rings through my brain, loud and clear.

Here's what I mean. It was 2015, and we were launching a chapter in Jordan. At the time, I was working a full-time gig and still moonlighting for Girls in Tech, so exhausted doesn't cut it. I came home every night feeling fried. Burned out to a crisp.

Now, normally at the events, I show up to get onstage and say a few words and shake the right hands. Remember, these events aren't about *me*, they're supposed to be about the local communities, the local businesses, the women volunteers who are dedicating much more time at the local level than I possibly can. As I understood it, this event was going to be a similar drill to previous versions: I'd say a few welcoming words, smile a lot, and then roll up my (red?) dress sleeves and get to work.

Like 99 percent of the human population, I excel at procrastination. I told myself to prepare something on paper. To write something down (*Be witty, damn it!*). To maybe do some research on local stats and start-ups. But remember, I was fried. Crispy. It just didn't happen.

Also, like a large part of the population, around-the-world flights give me jet lag and downgrade me to the hydration level of a freeze-dried berry. When I walked off that plane, I felt hung over without any of the fun the night before, completely disoriented and parched. *Fuck Up Part Deux.* Here's a tip: arrive to international events at least two days early.

The event was that day, so, unfortunately, I didn't have the luxury of a long bath or, better yet, a longer snooze. I freshened up and then off I was. I'd make the best of it . . . wouldn't I?

There was just (yet another) problem. This one I didn't discover until I was at the event and holding a frozen grin. The US ambassador to Jordan, Alice Wells, stood before me onstage and delivered a polished, inspirational, cohesive talk. She rallied the crowds. She grinned. Hell, she looked like she slept ten hours the night before! She spoke for at least ten or fifteen minutes. And she did it all in a way that made it look easy.

She was confident. She was *prepared*. And I was up next.

I had no idea I'd be following a professional pseudo-political speaker. But I had been told I'd get onstage, and I didn't listen. I stumbled up to the podium and nervously took hold of the mic (was that me shaking?).

"Good afternoon," I began. "Thank you, everyone, for coming today. My name is Adriana Gascoigne, and I'm founder and CEO of Girls in Tech."

Mind. Blank. *Shit.*

"Thank you for coming today. I'm so happy to be here. It's great to see so many women come here to support each other. We're going to have a great afternoon. The managing directors have put on a great event for you today."

I could see faces in the crowd. I could see them looking at each other. *Is this an American thing? Is this her first presentation, ever? She's nervous.* And then when they noticed I was nervous,

I became even more nervous. *Shit, I was nervous!* And not only that, I felt stupid. Like I didn't know what I was doing and that others had found me out. I could see people in the crowd zoning out before my eyes. Cell phones came out; the echo of phones vibrating hung in the air. I was losing Girls in Tech's supporters before the afternoon even kicked off.

I was supposed to speak for ten to fifteen minutes, but I couldn't even hold the stage for five. I winged it, spouting out some canned words about our programs and our mission. Stumbling along and feeling my way in the dark. And it wasn't that my job was hard—it wasn't. I just had to be gracious for F's sake. But I was so physically worn out, so jetlagged and de- hydrated that my mind felt like an old-school TV stuck on the fuzzy channel.

When I finished with my dump of a welcome speech, I care- fully stepped down from the stage. I moved slow. I didn't have a cane, but it would have worked at that moment. It would have felt right. I was lightheaded. Embarrassed. Defeated.

Yes, it was really *that terrible*. When I replay it in my head, my first instinct is to play a game and count how many times I use the word "great" but then I remember, that's *me* talking, that's *me* screwing up!

I prepare now. I'm by no means perfect, but I show up hav- ing done my homework. And even though it's been more than three years, that day still bothers me. It feels like an ugly bruise on my journey with Girls in Tech.

Confidence is learned, it's earned, it's something women at all levels continuously strive for. There is no university course on confidence; it's something that comes with time. With prac- tice. I see the faces in the crowd at the Catalyst Conference, the way attendees look up to the women who present onstage, the fierce, brash, experienced women leaders who command atten- tion purely through their presence. But here's the thing: many of them are probably nervous when they're up there—despite their twenty-plus years of experience on you. Many of these women have faced off with their own reflections in the mirror, battling imposter syndrome just like the rest of us. They're on a constant march to justify their existence, to justify their stature, and to justify all the good that's come their way because of their hard work. They've fought to get where they should be, and then they fight themselves once they get there.

Because—despite the confidence we earn—so often, it's inherently programmed within us to refuse to accept it. I've noticed that some women even feel shame because of it. Is there such a thing as too much confidence? I want to say no, but I can't say for sure. I don't know what that would feel like; I'm just not there yet.

When you work at it, remember, I'm working at it too. And if you see me sporting red, try to give me a break that day. I probably need it.

WHAT DID WE LEARN?

✓ **You're in charge of your story.**
  You're in charge of your life, your choices, your story. That includes the way it unfolds. It includes the way you justify things. This doesn't mean you should lie about your past, and it doesn't mean to BS your way through every job interview or start-up pitch meeting. But it does mean to take a step back and try to be a bit rational, versus emotional, about what may have happened in the past. If you try to look at yourself objectively, often there are darn good reasons why things did or did not go your way. You just must push aside some cobwebs (and crappy self-esteem) to get there.

✓ **You shouldn't be afraid of what you don't know.**

Go ahead, make Google your best friend if you haven't done so already. And then own it. It's comical—and just so *unnecessary*—to see start-up founders putting so much pressure on themselves to get every move right. Every little decision, every meeting, every interaction. Talk about an inefficient way to go through life! Sure, you're in charge, but who says you need to have all the answers? It's your job to hire people who are smarter than you to help you navigate through the ambiguity. And, second, own it if you don't know the way. You'll likely be surprised at how many humans—and search engines—are willing to help you out.

✓ **Find your confidence ammunition, and load up.**

Like I said, for me it's red. Power red. But what's it going to be for you? Find the thing that works for you, and run like hell with it. It could be an incredible night of sleep. It could be a power pose, a '90s rap song, your mom's cooking, or a chat with a best friend. We all have our thing. Discover yours and use it.

✓ **Always be prepared.**

When you prepare, you feel good. You feel like you know your shit (because you do!). You may even get excited about something that you typically dread, all thanks to feeling like you can truly take ownership and speak to something confidently. This goes for anything, a work project, a presentation, an interview. Just try to not present after a US ambassador, okay?

CHAPTER 11

The Pitch

AH, THE ELUSIVE pitch. Yet another element of start-ups that is completely oversexed and glorified, probably thanks to events like TechCrunch Disrupt. The pitch is where start-ups and theater comingle, where there's drama onstage, and the pressure to present well is almost explosive. Everything you've been dreaming about, working on under the hood, toiling the moonlight hours away on—well, it's suddenly public AF. There you are, standing naked before people who matter—who can (seemingly) define your destiny and change your course. You're vulnerable. You're being stared at, and your heart is beating outside of your body, right there on your sleeve, and you're either going to convince them that you're the master of your universe or that you're just another wannabe with a pitch deck.

There you have it. So, what's it going to be?

If tech dorks and start-ups had a sport, it would be pitching. *See you at the pitchfest, bitches!* It's the equivalent of a badass mic drop; if you're good at it, you probably steal the show and leave onlookers a bit lusty, dreamy. Their heads will spin, thinking,

Holy shit, that was fucking good. If you suck, well, they'll think, *That sucked.* (And, yes, it's that simple.)

Going to a pitch event in Silicon Valley is for commoners. Presenting at them, that's a level up. For all my sarcasm, I want to truthfully point out: these entrepreneurs who get onstage and flaunt their start-up and work hard to get us on their ca-boose—they're brave. This is what true leadership looks like. And perhaps that's the allure. So much of a pitch event spears at the core of entrepreneurship, that deep-set optimism and diamond-strength belief that they're onto something, something wonderful and good and worth sacrificing for. There's beauty in that vision, there's a desire to witness it—even if you aren't running to grab your checkbook to get in on their game. It's still a wonder.

And such is the mystery of pitching. Everyone wants to know how to do it and how to do it well, the secret sauce. Pitching is a given if you're going to start your own company. In fact, if you are doing it right, you pitch your face off all day long. You do it at your networking events, you do it to friends and family at Sunday supper, you do it on the BART, at the bank, in stuffy VC conference rooms, and onstage. Start your company, then start pitching. You're an instant traveling salesperson, knocking on imaginary doors up and down the valley, in the form of introductions, concise "elevator pitches," and scrawled across your LinkedIn and AngelList profiles. You're a founder—this is your job now.

I've seen a lot of pitches, and Girls in Tech hosts its very own pitch competition specifically for female-founded start-ups, AMPLIFY. It happens every fall in San Francisco, where a basement room gets crowded end to end with entrepreneurs, start-up employees, high-tech workers, VCs, and journalists. On our "stage"—really, a modest setup at the front of the room—ten start-ups fight for a small seed round and perhaps something more valuable—visibility. Recognition. Credibility.

Of course, Girls in Tech does a pitch night exclusively for female-led start-ups because of the obvious—the female founder community tends to get stomped all over and dismissed when it comes time to write a check. So, the idea behind AMPLIFY is to give them a platform to share the amazing projects they're working on and to be heard without interruption, competition, or distraction from the typical male-led start-ups. As we said on our banners last year, sometimes we have to build our own stairway to success.

Before start-ups make it to the stage, they must pass an application process and get a thumbs-up from a team of exclusive judges. They need to put some effort into applying, pulling together key data points, sharing their pitch deck with us—convincing the team that they're worthy, more so than the other hundreds of applicants—to hit the stage and pitch for ten minutes. After, they answer questions from our panel of judges.

I'm not going to shame any start-ups here, but I've seen start-up founders just freeze when they get to the stage. They lock up and lose charisma. Their speech becomes robotic, and they stumble through the introduction. I've seen the audience sort of hesitate in response to this falter, unsure how to act. I've seen teams mumble into the mic; drag their product pitch on and on as though it were being dragged down the street. It's cringe-worthy. It's uncomfortable.

These are not the winners. These people—they're good on paper, and that's the last stop.

I've also seen founders get up there and stroll with their hands on their hips, as if to say, *I deserve to be here, and you better listen because I've got something to say.* We listen. They take to the mic like they're Toastmasters champs. They start off with a story, they lure us in like we're fish, waiting to get swept up into their tale and sent down the river. And we're ready to go because, hell, we want to hear more. We can relate to them;

they tell the story in such a way that heads nod throughout the crowd. Faces break away from their text conversations; people in the back shut up and pay attention. These founders are prepared. Their confidence, it's vibrant and sparkling and demands you snap to it. *You don't want to miss this.*

These are the winners. And they may not be the next Uber or Airbnb, but they give us enough. Enough to *believe.* Enough to want to give back to them (Money! Laptops! Office space! Mentors!). Enough to want to follow them on Twitter and sign up for their newsletter and stay engaged. There's an urge, when you see such a pitch, to want to join in on their party, to come along for the fun. To not miss out because it means you could be missing something extraordinary. That's magic.

THE BIG BUCKS (VENTURE CAPITAL)

But there's the more formal side to the pitch process, beyond friends and family and the adrenaline of pitch competitions: the chase for venture capital. For start-ups that have true high-growth potential—with the ability to return millions and rapidly scale—venture capital is where it's at. Remember, VC isn't for every start-up (though it seems like most start-ups think it is). VC is for start-ups with industry-revolutionizing potential. It's all about market size and expected return. VCs will want their money back (and then at least ten times their investment!) in five to ten years. VC is appropriate for new technologies that are expected to return a billion dollars or more. These are companies that are pioneering new technologies with a massive growth opportunity. These are companies that aren't just taking over markets; they're creating new ones.

Ask yourself, Do you think your start-up can do it? Do the numbers support that level of return? Do your numbers make sense?

VC is not going to work for lifestyle companies that may do very well for themselves but not return that level of money. Restaurants. Small businesses. Consulting firms. Tech companies that simply don't have a large enough market opportunity. VCs aren't interested in the small change, they want to see massive ROI. Remember, they're betting millions that your company is going to do something radical. Big investments mean big expectations. It's not an insult if VC isn't right for you; it's an expectation founders need to be aware of. As you'll see, that may not be such a bad thing.

Pitching to VCs is like nothing else. It takes over your life. It will drive you *insane*, having you clawing at the walls, and potentially derail your life for several months. It becomes all consuming. Why? Conversations with VCs take time—there are simply a lot of them to be had. It's a process to go through. Applications and networking and coffee meetings and team meetings and spreadsheets. And you must go through it because you need money to survive. It's that simple: at some point, you're going to run out of your own cash, you're going to burn through all the seed money you've received from friends and family or a crowdsourced campaign, or you're going to have big plans that require big bucks to execute. You need money; even if you're frugal, you still need it to operate.

Raina Kumra, a dear friend of mine, served as cofounder of Mavin, an international mobile start-up. Their goal was to create an affordable internet by making access easy. Raina's background is in marketing, branding, and design. She's worked with the likes of Disney and the US government on brand strategy, so she's no novice when it comes to the value of a well-defined brand and the value of a first impression. She and I spoke about her experience fundraising as a first-time founder. At the time, Mavin had raised a solid seed round of more than $2 million, and they had just closed on their series A.

Raina knew pitching was going to be a tough process. But she was still blown away by the experience.

"It was shockingly not what I expected. VCs were not the thoughtful, smart personalities I thought I'd be encountering," she said. "For the majority, I was unimpressed. I lost a lot of respect for this field that has all this razzle and dazzle around it, because everyone wants to be a VC. Everyone wants to talk to VCs. Everyone wants to get funding from them. But after my first thirty to forty conversations, I was like, I would much rather take a business loan or take a friends and family loan than take money from some of these people."

Egos. She ran into egos. And just a heck of a lot of dead ends, probably what a lot of job seekers experience when they are in full-blown job-hunt mode. You reach out to a LOT of companies, and no one gets back to you. Raina experienced this. Many VCs wouldn't give her an answer, period. And those who did—well, they seemed to count themselves as a super-elite polite bunch for simply responding. For Raina, this was incredibly frustrating—there she was raising money, dedicating all her time to the process, but often unable to close the door on conversations because of this lack of communication. More time down the drain.

Plus, she was shocked by the lack of risk appetite. When you think of a VC, you think of a gambler, someone who is willing to take a risk, perhaps even a dreamer who can quickly pick up on new models, emerging markets, and life-changing concepts.

But Raina said that she noticed a bit of a herd mentality among VCs. "They just really wanted to invest in super safe models that they already knew existed and worked. We were working on something that has a social impact. It has a deep systems effect. For all these people who say that they want something world changing, they could not be more disinterested in emerging markets. That was also shocking. Most of the VCs in

Silicon Valley only care about Silicon Valley. They always are trying to invest in the Uber of 'blank.'"

She was fine with having repeat conversations to help educate the skeptics. And, for many, she did. In fact, she relied on education to help get her over the hump. But she also tried to explore outside the traditional bucket of VCs to break away from the low risk tolerance. For example, she explored family investment offices. These paths put Raina and her team in front of people who seemed to understand what they were doing far more quickly and intuitively than VCs.

Not to really drag this conversation down even further, but I'll point out what many of you readers may suspect by now: that gorgeous pitch deck that you spend hours and hours and hours on? Whelp. Raina noticed that many VCs didn't even hit the open button. She knows this for a fact because she could see in her electronic signature software dashboard just how many (er, few) seconds were spent on her pitch materials. Seconds that you can count on one hand, mind you.

Although it's important to remember that this was just one experience, I'm sharing it with you so that you can be prepared . . . to possibly be disappointed.

"They read maybe the first two pages," she said. *Sigh.*

But, despite that, Raina's inner marketer knows that the pitch deck still must be flawless. It's an important element in your quest for cash; it must be well designed (hint: hire someone!), slick. Impressive. This is not the area to get crafty and do-it-yourself.

"The pitch deck is your five-second ad. You only get five seconds to make an impression."

Okay, so this process doesn't sound awesome, does it? Raina said she went through seventy-nine meetings and had seventy-four "no" responses and five "yes" responses. Damn. But they did it because they had to. Mavin required a lot of cash—it needed to purchase mobile data packets to keep its business churning. That left the company without the option to get super-gritty and bootstrap. Raina said that even with a low valuation and "expensive money" from a VC, she and her fellow founders agreed quickly that raising VC outweighed the personal risk of burning through their personal funds.

Despite her jaunt through fundraising hell, Raina did wind up quite pleased with her investors. Initially, they were hoping for investors who would sort of stay on the sidelines—give 'em money and then let them get to work. However, they realized that investors who are true partners are best—those who can fight the fight alongside them.

"We wanted people who would be there long term through all the pivots," she said. "Who understood the mission. Trusted us." She says she did find them—active investors who get it and believe in their idea—and that they are "really happy" with them. So, it looks like her perseverance paid off.

✳

Okay, so we know fundraising is a road paved with potholes, egos, and rejection. And we know we need a pitch deck, but what makes a perfect pitch?

That's what every entrepreneur is attempting to unlock. "If you knew the secret sauce, everyone would use it, and, by defi-nition, it wouldn't work anymore," Heidi Roizen, serial entre-preneur and venture partner at DFJ, said.

Heidi has seen countless pitches. Although she can't point to a specific formula for success, she notes that storytelling plays a role in the good ones. And she points out that successful pitches tend to share a common story arc.

For example, this is a generic pitch template Heidi suggests:

I was doing X: *I worked in product management in the hospi-tality industry for more than 10 years.*

I became very good at doing X: *We did extensive field testing and launched numerous lucrative partnerships.*

But, over and over again, I saw people struggle with Y: *I saw customers consistently have issues booking flights. They couldn't find a deal, and then the seats would always sell out.*

X did not solve for Y: *My employer didn't have the resources or software knowledge to tackle the problem. And, at the time, no one else in the space had a compelling flight deals website.*

I came up with this compelling way of solving Y: *I made a deals app myself, and I launched in three US cities last year.*

People will pay a ton of money to solve this problem: *In six months alone, we grew to more than 1 million users.*

Here's why I am uniquely qualified to solve this problem: *I have key contacts throughout the travel industry and with all the major airlines. I have a built-in network that has guaranteed to offer my company exclusive deals that people can find nowhere else.*

Here's why one hundred people are not trying to solve this problem right now: *The travel industry tends to come with tight margins and a lot of customer-service pain points. My company bypasses these issues by focusing on exclusive, limited-time offers, available only through a mobile app.*

"It's the power of a story format, the power of being able to bring someone along," Heidi said. "We are humans, we are storytellers. I do believe having the element of a story is very important in a great pitch."

The template above hits the main points. But remember to back your story up with data to pack it with a bit of a punch. You outline the problem. But how many people experience this problem? What does this problem cost people? Why does this problem matter? You outline why you're the person who can solve it. Do you have some sort of patented technology? Are you connected to key suppliers that most folks can't connect to? Are you one of the brightest minds in the world to solve this problem?

A pitch can and should include all the key points that you want to tout but in a boiled down version. You may want a slide on key milestones you've hit to date, your other team members, why your technology is exceptional. You may want logos of early clients in the deck, if they are well known and worth bragging about. You'll probably want to include a slide that shows what you know about your target customers—who are they, how many of them are out there, what do they care about? This is a ten- to twenty-slide deck that gives you the chance to put forth all your top points in a buttoned-up, kid-simplistic communication style. Spoon-feed it to investors, hold their hands, and guide them to see what you see.

※

Presentation matters. I'm talking about the way you speak to investors and customers and journalists about your business. Take it from Jessica Scorpio, founder and chief marketing officer at Getaround, a wildly ambitious car-sharing start-up. Not ride sharing, *car* sharing. You are making your car available to people who need to "get around" by using its platform, and you're essentially handing the keys to your wheels over to a stranger. Crazy, right? Yes. Crazy. Wild. Ambitious. Aspirational. And spot-fucking-on. The idea is to have a global impact, to promote the concept of sharing pricy resources such as cars, and to change a lot of lives. Thousands of lives, millions of lives.

Jessica is perfect to ask about pitching because she militantly prepared for Getaround's TechCrunch Disrupt NYC pitch in 2011. Talk about theatrics! A huge (intimidating) conference. Press. Investors. Pressure oozing from every cell. Getaround chose to debut with flair and anticipation, a go-big-or-go-home approach. Another team could have flopped, but this one *prepared* as if everything depended on it—and it showed. It paid off. Jessica and I spoke about her TechCrunch debut but also about what she's learned from raising money overall; when we spoke, she was chasing after her C round.

"In some ways it gets easier. If you have a good process, you learn in the earlier stages and then you get better each time," she said. "We learned that different raises have different expectations and preparations and challenges. . . . Series C expects a lot more data, a totally different amount of diligence."

But, she notes, start-ups should be thinking about these changing expectations from the start. Whereas your seed and A rounds may be more about the concept and the brand and the story, you need to be collecting data and doing testing early on (here's looking at you, product management folks!) so that you have ammo in your back pocket for when you go on to raise later rounds.

That's not the only thing that changes round to round. Jessica noted that the environment will keep changing. You may raise one round in an economic downturn, another round when things are hot. She referred to it as an "interesting checkerboard" of patterns. So, you can be prepared each time with data, with a story, and the perfect pitch, but just be aware that the environment overall may be drastically different—and that's something that's out of your control. Getaround persevered through several ups and downs in the market because—ta da!—it needed the money; its IP and technology are not cheap to develop.

In many ways, Jessica's early process with venture capitalists mirrors Raina's.

"We got some comments like, 'I would never even share my car with my wife!' she reflected. "Some VCs can't grasp that they're not the target market. There are tons of products out there. They're like, '*Oh we don't use this stuff.*' But there's the rest of the world. I think for a lot of them, it was a real leap of faith; they couldn't wrap their head around why someone would want to share their car."

An interesting parallel to Raina's struggle with getting VCs to grasp the company's vision and see the benefits and understand the value, no? This is a core challenge with the lack of diversity at the VC level. So many of these firms look the same: one white guy after the other. They all have a shitload of money. They all eat at the same types of restaurants, live in similar big, gorgeous houses, drive the same lines of luxury cars. They can't break away from their own lives to understand what real people need and want. That is, until the likes of a Snapchat comes along to make them think twice.

And then, fundraiser beware: Jessica warns that if you do make it to a term sheet, approach it with caution. VCs, she said, are incredibly self-interested. You're going to be excited and you're going to want to just say *yes!* and shout it from the rooftops, and take the sheet and sign and run with it. There's going to be an urge to celebrate and call it a day.

But these term sheets—and all these complex financial terms and numbers, this likely isn't your niche. Don't assume the best. Have your eyes wide open. You may be getting played, and many VCs will work hard to convince you that they're delivering the best deal possible to you, when signing could lead to catastrophic consequences. You're vulnerable. You're emotional. And they know it.

They also know each other, and they're tightly networked in the valley. Jessica has heard of deals where they're buddies with someone, term sheets get taken away, or there are backdoor deals where much higher percentages of the company get doled out.

"You have to be a good negotiator and really calm under pressure because they're going to convince you that this is the last thing for you. That this is the only way to succeed. You're going to have to decide who you really want to work with."

Because, when VCs are taking 20 to 30 percent of your company—*your company*—it's a big deal who you work with. Find a partner, not a manipulator. One way to do this is to talk to other founders. Ask to speak with company founders that are in their current portfolio. Do a bit of amateur investigating and look into their reputation. Are they honest? Do they come through with what they say? Who is angry with them or super happy with them?

This is a good time to point out that you're going to need an experienced attorney. Don't screw around with this, and don't attempt to negotiate through a term sheet (and for fuck's sake—do not sign!) without an experienced, reputable attorney, one who has dealt with countless VCs before. This person will guide you through the process, catch the small print (the small print that could bring you to the ground), and stick up for you when you don't even know your chain is being pulled.

Jessica and her team chose to launch at TechCrunch Disrupt to maximize their visibility. They were a tiny team—four people, with her as the only main full-time person at the time. Early-stage start-ups can get lost in the web of wanting to do it all: get press coverage, speak with investors, polish their presentation, develop their product, and so on. But you can't do it all. Jessica and her team knew this, and so they chose to exclusively obsess about the presentation of their demo.

This meant practice. A lot of it. Over and over and over again. They practiced questions and answers with anyone who would listen. They even hired a speaking coach. They went through the process exhaustively, leaving nothing to chance. And—as Jessica puts it—they "nailed the presentation." The judges went apeshit over Getaround. People came to them to ask how to get involved and how to invest.

There they were, a tiny team of four. Hot and competitive and strewn across the headlines.

A year later, Getaround posted a guest article to TechCrunch, outlining its key tips for how to conquer Disrupt. They advise investing in a great PR team (it's worth the money!). And—because you get only six minutes onstage—to get right to your demo within forty-five seconds. Also, have someone drive your presentation for you (in other words, don't have the speaker up onstage, fumbling through the deck or losing track of time).[1]

Does this make it real now? Look at the sheer amount of time that needs to go into a pitch—in this case, a wee little six-minute presentation. Serious founders can't wing the pitch process. Don't rely on your charm or connections to see you through. In this case, you need to be a perfectionist. Become obsessive. Practice and practice again, and don't assume you have it right, even up to the minute you walk onstage to deliver the message.

Getaround's payoff for all the hard work: "We went from this crazy idea to tech scene start-up sweetheart. We got thousands of sign-ups all in the same day. We had 5,000 car leads, in one day. I think at the time we only had 5,000 cars total. We thought, we're totally onto something here. There is demand for this."

(Do you have a total urge to high-five the Getaround team, like I do?)

*

Pitching is a skill founders and non-founders alike can leverage throughout their lifetime. Don't underestimate its value. Girls in Tech doesn't seek venture capital—we're not the right fit, being a nonprofit—but we pitch ourselves several times a week, every week. My team and I are constantly in meetings with mammoth-sized global corporations, touting what we can do for them, how we can get creative and partner together—like help them diversify their workforce and create a more inclusive culture. I use start-up-style pitching in these meetings, every week. And just like start-ups and the dang pitch deck, we have our own version too.

To be able to communicate with finesse and precision—to win over a crowd and persuade—will never fail you.

Know your story. Get good at telling it with confidence and ease and simplicity, whether you're a founder, an intrapreneur, or a smart woman looking for her next career move.

WHAT DID WE LEARN?

✓ **There's nothing sexy about pitching.**
The process of pitching is nothing like the end result. It's like how people will say pregnancy is so beautiful and sexy. Yep, it looks that way from the outside, but friends tell me the truth—about the tearing, the hemorrhoids, varicose veins, and new body hair. But no one wants to hear about that, right? It's the same way with pitching. It looks badass from afar, even fun. But behind the scenes there's a team of founders who become compulsive about every edit to their pitch deck, who tremble before they walk onstage. Who tuck their rosary into their blouse in hopes that their product doesn't fail upon demo.

And then there's the shitty reality about pitching—about the vast number of companies you're going to speak with that just don't care about you. They won't understand your product. They just can't get through their mental block that says, "Gee, I'd never use that, I don't see why people would pay for that."

It's a cycle of talking, presenting, rejection. It's going to get into your head, and it's going to bruise you from the inside out.

✓ Plan to be distracted.

It's also going to take over your life. Founders who have been there, done that will likely have more discipline in not letting this happen (too much). Even though you need money and you need to prioritize fundraising, you still must painstakingly push your product forward and hit your release deadlines and test and sell.

Start-ups aren't linear. You don't do one thing and then another, like a neat row of dominoes falling down the line. Fundraising and pitching take an already complex and stressful process and shake it around like a snow globe. Try to set aside specific hours in your day, or days in your week, to work on pitching. Manage expectations with your team about who needs to do what and how available you will be, or won't be, throughout the process.

✓ Your pitch deck needs to say, *"We know our shit."*

Oh, the irony: few people will read your pitch deck entirely, yet it needs to be absolutely perfect. Perfect. You'll get many conflicting opinions about how to make it that way. Everyone is going to have an idea, down to your color and font choice.

And although you can't just change based on everyone's tiny little whim, take the feedback seriously. Take your deck seriously. This is not a time to get halfhearted in your work ethic.

✓ **Exhaustively practice. And then do it again. And again.**
Many entrepreneurs treat meetings like just another casual coffee date. But if you're meeting with an investor, put your game face on. Give yourself a kick in the booty.

Getaround's approach should serve as something to strive for. Creating the perfect pitch—with all the detail and all the theatrics—takes a ton of time, dedication, and discipline. It's going to be a lot of pain but also a lot of payback. Look at it like an investment.

✓ **Reach for the stars but be grounded in reality.**
Founders are optimists by nature—we were born that way. But don't think you're going to get funding from the start. You may go through thirty meetings . . . eighty meetings . . . a hundred meetings. Be realistic about the time that is going to go into those meetings. Put on your kneepads, because you're going to be rejected over and over again. Don't let it beat you down too much. You'll come out okay on the other side—but just know that you might have to go through VC hell to get there.

CHAPTER 12

Leadership

SO, WHAT DO you do after some of the fundamentals are in place, like a possible cofounder, a team, or investment dollars? You're going to be expected to take charge. *Lead*.

Start-up leadership is a peculiar thing, because leadership is typically a learned art, whittled and sanded and refined throughout your career. It's something that even the most revered leaders—the ones you see onstage, the supposed unreachables, the ones you admire from afar—consistently study and work to perfect. And the better you are, the more likely you are to never ever check it off your list. You're never done learning how to lead your team; you can only hope you get better as you go.

You can take all the management classes you want in college, but, much like real-world business acumen and skills like networking and negotiation, you're not going to know a thing until you do it, with your feet on the coals and your butt in the hot seat. It's easy to say you're the CEO. It's easy to say you want to lead a team, that you'll be that "cool boss" and that you have things under control. Until you aren't, until you don't.

Which is why start-up leadership can be okay, or it can be total shit. Of course, not all start-up leaders are young, but many are. And what happens when you get a bunch of twenty-somethings with a C-suite title? There's a good chance it's like watching kids play a game of "house." They're sweeping pretend floors, baking plastic cupcakes, and sporting a chef's hat and apron like it's Disneyland. It's not that the drive to be a good leader isn't there but rather that the tools and experience are missing.

I'm sure this is insulting to many start-up leaders in their twenties, but, hey, I used to be you. I can say this. I know what it's like to start something and to feel like I'm the shit because I have "founder" in my e-mail footer. I know the apprehensive excitement that you feel when you design your first logo; that logo feels like the most important part of your business—it's your crown jewels, your calling card, everything you want associated with you and your face and your new biz. It feels so grown up and official. I know how important you feel when you hire someone for the first time. (Who's the boss? You da boss!)

Don't act like these things haven't gone through your head. I know. And I've spoken to enough founders, witnessed enough founders, to know that these are the currents that run through the start-up pool, and we all wade in these waters. I'm just a little more upstream now. And I should add, even older founders who have totally switched career gears with their start-up can struggle with this (not just young folks).

So, start-ups: the pressure is on and you have to rapidly grow and you're in charge, yet you don't know what you're doing. You've been thrown onto a basketball court, yet you're the five-foot-three dude in XXL shorts who loses the ball. And everyone is turning to you for answers. What do you do? Do you approach your team members like it's their royal blessing or do you tell your ego to go for a walk and try to be human?

I think you know the answer. Let me rephrase that. I think you know the answer about what you *should* do.

HEAR IT FROM A VETERAN LEADER

Let's take it from Meg Withgott, founder and CTO of Panafold, a San Francisco–based start-up. She hails from the early days at Xerox PARC, Interval, and Sun Labs. She's also an investor through Golden Seeds, both professionally and personally. We're lucky to have had Meg speak at Catalyst and to count her as an avid supporter of women in tech. You don't have to know Meg long to get a sense of her deep appreciation for imagination, ideas, the roots of innovation, and (lucky you) a refreshing perspective on what it takes to lead a team.

When we spoke about this book, Meg had leadership on her mind. She wanted to talk about the attitude of a leader—how do you approach the role if you're in the driver's seat at a young company?

"Maybe you're the CEO and you have this fancy title, but you have it for the first time so it's kind of scary. And maybe you have a model, like 'I should be just like Mark Zuckerberg.' But that's not who you are, and you probably don't know what he's like anyway. So, how do you keep your team inspired and keep true to yourself?"

One approach Meg suggests for founders is to consider how they start their day with their team. The start of the day sets the pace. Imagine, she said, an old-fashioned horse-drawn wagon. Someone needs to hold the reins. However, if people know that you hold the reins, they'll have expectations about how things will unfold. And it's up to you as the leader to set that rhythm. "You can set the rhythm in an enjoyable way," she said. "Start with a win. For example, always be ready to show something. I've seen this done in many successful organizations."

Here's what she means. Rather than retreat to a corner and get stressed out, you can bring the team together in a very positive way—right out of the gate, every morning. Set the tone for the day. Set the tone for what will feel normal for the day, for how you'll drive productivity. Ask everyone to have something to show, even if it's a small win. Not only will this help drive team satisfaction, it also guarantees you're always on top of it. If someone wants to see a demo later in the day or you receive an unexpected visitor, you're always prepared. You can think of it as progress but also consider it the day's inspiration.

"As a young leader to think of yourself as orchestrating a team, it's a privilege. But it doesn't have to be like a drill sergeant. It's up to you to set the rhythm and the tone. You think you will get more respect if you act mean or angry, and that people will respect you more. But it's usually the opposite. I think it's always a mistake to try to stress people into productivity."

Speaking of stress, how you manage it—and your team's reaction to it—is an important part of the leadership gig. You're in the grips of tremendous pressure; you're going to respond to stress in certain ways while the individuals on your team may respond in entirely different ways. Rather than getting frustrated with these differences, Meg noted that it's an opportunity to learn about each other as human beings.

"There's probably more cultural diversity in a team than you realize as a young leader. Backgrounds explain a lot. What are the triggers? What are the working styles?" What's considered offensive in one culture may be acceptable in another. Having some understanding of the cultural nuances within your team can help you ride out the bumps and come out the other side as an interconnected, supportive team.

"If you don't know what people's expectations are in moments of stress, your team will revert to what they *think* they should be doing. People will start talking past each other. It would be funny if it weren't so tragic. Having an understanding of cultural nuances ahead of those times is useful."

Tech CEOs don't typically come with a degree in anthropology or intrapersonal communications. And asking people upfront about their communication styles won't necessarily work, either, for the same reasons. ("It's like fish, they don't know they're in water," Meg said.)

However, most tech CEOs *do* come with a pair of sturdy ears. Meg said listening—just being there to listen and to ask questions—is a good starting point when you're dealing with an upset team member, especially because you probably don't have an HR department. Sure, you may have to listen to someone who needs to vent. And perhaps that goes against your style of dealing with the highs and lows of start-up life, but venting may be something this person *needs to do.* And it's your job to be there. And to listen.

Put your phone on silent and tuck it away. Put this team member front and center. Ask questions. *Why are you upset? What are you angry about? What has you worried?* Don't be condescending; just ask.

Here's the heart of why this really matters: "You can have a great product. You can have funding. But if your team goes sideways, you have to start all over again."

ASSHOLES

I'm not going to pretend I'm not one of those leaders who is all set and polished, and not still fumbling for their horse-drawn carriage reins in the dark. I'm not perfect, no arguing there, but I've learned quite a few things in my ten-plus years running this organization.

The biggest thing that I apply in my daily leadership practice and something I try to drive home with every team member is this: don't be an asshole.

I wish I could say that I came up with that myself, but I didn't. Robert Sutton coined the phrase when he wrote a book about working with nasty people—how to survive it, strategies for getting through it. (It's fittingly titled *The No Asshole Rule: Building a Civilized Workplace and Surviving One That Isn't*.) Assholes can ruin a start-up environment in particular. Unlike large enterprises with hundreds or thousands of people to hide among, an asshole at a start-up of, say, ten people or fewer can do a lot of damage. In those cases, they can be unwaveringly toxic.

I never thought I would say that a book with the word "asshole" on its cover inspired me, but that one did. After I read the book, I informally adopted its rule for Girls in Tech. The point: to embed a culture of respect within Girls in Tech and everything we touch, to avoid demeaning people. And, honestly, I just wanted to avoid drama. Isn't that something we all want?

This also falls heavily in line with my lessons learned from bad hiring. I'm no longer that chick that blindly trusts. Now, I go into new work relationships with a big heart and eyes wide open. It begins in the interview process. Is a candidate rude, arrogant, combative? If so, that should be it. She may be the most talented developer on the planet, but it's not worth bringing her on if she is going to set fire to the amazing culture you've nurtured from day one.

Next, get ready to confront an A-hole if necessary. Bullies are bullies until they're called out on their bullshit. You may have to use this outside your organization, with anyone from a vendor to a VC or a partner. Assholes live and work everywhere, and with the egos you'll experience when you build your start-up, don't assume that you're going to have an issue on the inside. In fact, your biggest problems may actually lie with outsiders.

For example, I've had people who have tried to come to me under the guise of partnership, who have told me they want to work with me in cofounder roles—only to have them try to steal intellectual property, swoop up Girls in Tech domains or logos and run with them. I've had people try to get me to sign off on legal documents that are suspiciously all-encompassing. I've had partners who aren't sincerely trying to do right by women or increase their company diversity but fall more within the lines of just trying to say they contributed to a "women's organization" and call it a day. That doesn't work. All of this doesn't work. And I've had to walk away from what I thought were great opportunities, big checks, or global partnerships. If it's not right, it's not right.

Here's the kicker: the biggest part of this rule is just getting into the habit of trusting your gut. Don't think you're pushed into a corner. Don't fall into the trap of believing you don't have options elsewhere. You always have a choice, in everything you do and in every person you work with.

DO THE RIGHT THING

Another thing about me—and, admittedly, this may be less of a leadership thing and more about the warm fuzzies—is I like flowers. I like surprises. I like doing *nice things* for people. I frequently try to do nice things for my team members to make them feel appreciated. I don't think any management textbook tells you to send flowers to thank someone, or to tell team members to just take a day if they are sick, or to occasionally treat them to a spa day, but these things happen in my book.

We're overworked, we're a tiny bunch, and we're working in a digital, high-stress world. I believe health is everything. I try to step back and decompress when I need to (so I can be a better leader), but I also try to cascade this practice to my team. Turns out, you get a lot more work done, and you're in a better mood when you've gotten sleep the night before! And I haven't bothered with an official experiment, but flowers seem to be good bang for the buck—they really make someone's day. Go figure.

Also, something I started a few years ago, in line with de-compressing and health: an organizational retreat. The first year we went to the hills of southern France, next we're headed to Costa Rica. This isn't just a retreat for my corporate work team, it's an opportunity for global managing directors who lead in-dividual Girls in Tech chapters, as well as our board members to join in. That means women from all over the world fly in to spend three or four incredible days together, women from all corners of the world. It's our annual opportunity, beyond the Catalyst Conference, to see each other in person. To really connect, to look each other in the eye, to ditch our phones for a while. We hike, we meditate, we take cooking classes. There's yoga, wine, star-gazing, and a white party.

It's an investment: there's the hotel and the workshops. But I believe it's critically important to bring everyone together physically. We've grown exponentially in the past several years, and one of the challenges is to maintain a sense of friendship the world over, and guiding our culture and values from a co-working space in San Francisco offers up challenges, even with the best in technology and collaboration tools.

I'm not saying start-ups need to start booking international trips or looking up connections to a travel agency. But I would suggest that start-up founders think of small but significant ways that they can invest in themselves and their team. This is the humblest part of leadership, acknowledging that you wouldn't be anywhere—that you'd be nothing—without your team. So, go on, tell your team that they rock. Tell them to leave early on a Friday after a particularly grueling workweek. Host a happy hour. Say thank you (no flowers necessary, but eye contact re-quired). Buy them a meaningful book.

And above all, listen to them.

Most of these things don't cost money, but they mean some-thing. You're acknowledging hard work, dedication, loyalty, and tenacity. And sometimes this is all people need in order to want to stick it out with you for a long while, if you're lucky.

WHAT DID WE LEARN?

✓ **You set the tone for the day, every day.**
You're in charge! Expect your team to know this, to feel this, and to expect you to provide some guidance. But being a leader doesn't mean you need to be bossy or bully your team into action. You have a choice: you can be a bitch about it, or you can be a nice person to work for. The latter is going to result in happier, more productive employees. People want to work for nice people. This means trying to de-stress (before you pass it on to your team), being realistic about expectations and guidelines, and setting the tone for a "Go Team!" mentality every day.

✓ **Listening is an essential skill.**
I'm assuming you don't have an HR department. I'm assuming you're not a life coach or therapist for your side gig. But, as a leader, you must be prepared to wear any and all hats, including chief listener. Your team needs to see that you understand what it is going through—the pressure, the stress, the exhaustion. Listening doesn't cost money, but it does cost time. Be committed to shove other priorities (including your flashing, shining phone) to the side to make it happen.

✓ **Just say no to assholes.**
Start-up life is tough enough without working with annoying, angry, unhappy people. So, just don't do it. You do have a choice, remember? This goes for leaders and employees. Enough with excuses (*but I needed a job . . . but we couldn't*

find any other developer . . . but we had to hire someone that week). Enough. That one decision, to work with someone or not—which seems so flighty, so insignificant at the time—can literally change the course of your start-up for better or for worse. The people you work with will break you or make you.

✓ Make an investment.

If you're a leader and you're surrounded by incredible people, you want to keep it that way. You don't need to woo them with Tiffany's jewelry, but you do need to make an investment, with your time. Stop thinking about yourself and express appreciation for your team through thoughtful gestures. A half day off, a wellness day, a happy hour, taking a meeting in a park—these things are the currency of a happy work environment. But unfortunately, many first-time leaders can't get past their own power trip and egos to see it.

CHAPTER 13

Failure

IN 2013, I was living in Singapore. I had been there for a few years, and, through mutual friends, I became acquainted with a man seeking a cofounder for his online education company. My heart tugged at the opportunity: it would be my first experience as a true cofounder, rather than a founding team member. And I would have the champion title, CEO. Here was an opportunity to have heavy-weight equity, end-to-end ownership, and to be at the helm of an exciting start-up with massive potential. Something I could call mine, a business I could shape as I see fit. It was too good to pass up.

It lasted eight months. Eight months later, I was packing my bags for my return trip to the United States, and it wasn't just for a visit. I was returning for good.

WHAT FAILURE FEELS LIKE

Failure, an ugly word. An uncomfortable word. The irony is that many Silicon Valley types try to lacquer it up, slap some lipstick on it, and make it feel like a gold star. You don't have to live here to have heard something along the lines of failure being a sort of "badge of honor" or "it's okay to fail here" or "everyone fails and it's okay."

Here we go. Our whole life we strive for success, to make ourselves happy. To please our parents. To earn smiles and good grades from our teachers. To get those degrees, network our way into our dream careers, fight for a lineup of achievements we can tout on LinkedIn or AngelList. And then, in the same breath, the idea of failure—that *thing* we've been taught to avoid—gets cheerleaders and slogans and a bunch of other happy shit? What's next, its own logo and PR representation?

I don't buy it. Failure isn't something to tout, and it's not something to treat like it's a reward chart win. Unfortunately, this is business, not potty training.

And, besides, I'm allowed to be cynical. I know what failure is like, and it's not a day at the spa.

And failure can be public. High up there on the mantel for all to see. It can be an excruciating source of shame, like you have a secret to hide, even from yourself. It's that story you don't want to talk about, the junk you shove in the closet before company comes to visit and you want to make it look like your cleaning lady just left. It's the conversation you awkwardly want to avoid, where your laugh is a little high-pitched and you insist you're okay. Where you laugh a bit too hard, you insist a bit too long. And people can see right through your amateur monologue.

It's embarrassing. It's the toilet paper that trails after you've left the ladies' room at a five-star hotel. *Well, we know where she's been.* It's that thing you've run your mouth about—that big plan, that big mission, that big goal—that you just couldn't pull off. *You.* Just couldn't pull off. *You.* Screwed things up.

It's personal. And it doesn't go away, not immediately. Failure hovers in your shadows, trailing behind your personal brand like a taunt, a bullyish hiss. It takes every good feeling you have and every win and all the things you thought you were—all the good ones—and it kicks them squarely in the shins. Everyone in Silicon Valley has failed . . . right? Most start-ups fail . . . right? You try to reassure yourself with the facts, but it's hard to feel like you have company. Yes, in a city where thousands and thousands of failures occur every day, you feel lonelier and shittier and more incompetent than ever. It's completely illogical, but suddenly you look around you and see start-ups thriving left and right. You see entrepreneurs raising rounds. Acquisitions occurring. Of course, other start-ups are failing too and you're not alone, but it doesn't matter. During these times, logic goes out the window. When you break up, you see the world as a sea of couples. When you run your start-up into the ground, you see the world filled with thriving businesses.

Even now, failure is a shitty thing to discuss, and maybe that's why I need to do it here. Because although I don't buy into the idea that failure is something to flaunt, I do think it helps to share it honestly with others, which is what I'm going to do here. The truth is that many of us *do* experience it, and a little commiserating can help. So here it is, just me and these pages and my truth. (And you, reader. Just don't tell anyone, okay? Pinky swear.)

THAT ONE TIME I FAILED

Singapore.

The start-up was an e-learning platform designed to help small- and medium-sized businesses learn everything about online advertising and other promotional tools. Our aim was to handhold these business owners through online learning and make advertising easy, affordable, and accessible to thousands. It was a big opportunity, especially in the Asian market, where there was still quite a learning curve when it came to online advertising.

As I mentioned, I had been in Singapore for a few years working at various start-ups. By now, I was fairly entrenched in the tech scene there and well networked. A friend introduced me to the start-up's founder, and, over the course of a few months, we did a little dance around each other, exploring the idea of partnering.

We looked like we could be a good team. I understood he would bring significant resources to the table, including capital and connections to investors who would be valuable down the road. I understood he had already established relationships with dedicated developers, sales folks, marketing, you name it. He was to have 51 percent equity and I'd get 49 percent. Nothing to hang my head about. This was his baby from the start, and I was coming in to lead the team, manage the day to day, and see this thing take off. Dream team.

It was understood that he'd be more in the background but provide ample support. In other words, I'd have a treasure chest of resources to tap into but would get to run the show as far as decision making. Even now, looking back, it was a great deal, a very appealing opportunity.

But.

I'm sure you can see where this is going. Everything I expected from my cofounder, well, I only saw a sliver of it. It began quickly after I came on board.

Those developers? They couldn't get me too far—they were very basic resources, very limited. Suddenly, the budget became far smaller than I was led to believe when we shook hands. And, although I thought he'd be managing a lot of the operations, I was left on my own to deal with hiring, firing, HR and legal administration, finding more development resources, and so on.

You know that three- or four-year burnout that founders feel? For me, it was hitting at the four- and five-month mark. I felt as though I had stepped into a circus, but one I wasn't aware I'd be attending, where I was given a front-row seat and pulled unwillingly onto stage. My health visibly suffered; there I was, on the other side of the world and operating with a robotic mind-set. Sleep. Wake. Work. Work. Work. Sleep. Wake. Eat? Wait, did I eat? Work. Work. Work.

You get it. I wasn't okay. I was a shell. And what made it even worse is that I was a shell leading a shell of a company— one with a great concept and a supportive board, but nothing up our sleeve. No tools in our box.

I became angry, resentful. *Fuck this guy to leave me to deal with this—alone.* This was no partnership; it was a sham. I felt like he had pulled me into something blindfolded. The feeling was suffocating; I couldn't shake the idea that I had been trapped. At the same time, because I had less equity than he did, he could still trump my decisions from behind the scenes, even though I was left to deal with any consequences in person.

I was CEO, with nothing at my disposal, making chump change in an expensive city. It didn't smell right. And it sure as hell didn't feel right. All the good that I thought would be, all the excitement, all the upward movement—it wasn't happening. I knew, long before I cared to admit it to the world outside my own mind and heart, that I wasn't going to last the three- to four-year period I had committed to. I couldn't do it; I wouldn't survive it.

So I ran.

I told the board and my cofounder in one swoop. I sent one communication, explaining my challenges and that I needed to step back. I didn't hold back; I let them know that I had tried to uphold my end of the deal. *Not enough resources . . . no development team . . . can't do this.*

To the board's credit, they were shocked but remained respectful. Immediately, they had questions about the future of the company, next steps, who would be doing what. I referred them to my cofounder for answers. It wasn't unusual for an expat to want to go home, for it not to be a total fit. But, still, I was going home very soon, just shy of a year, a good bit shy of the long run that a new start-up needs from its leadership team. I was aware of this. Acutely aware of this.

And I knew I wanted to avoid drama. I readily gave up all 49 percent of my equity, my feeble gesture of goodwill and partnership, perhaps an effort to sneak out the back of the room unnoticed.

Three weeks later, I was on a plane, bound for the States. There was no elation, more like a failure hangover.

I felt all the ways I described above—the pit in the stomach, the shame, the loneliness. And then there was this: a terrible pit of anxiety that people would look at me differently. That investors would never want to take a chance on me again. That I was done for.

A FRESH BEGINNING

So there it is. I took my turn at failure, as though it's a carnival ride you get in line for. It's now many moons later, and I can talk about it in a better light. It stings less. Hindsight is certainly a gorgeous thing. But I'm not going to be bragging about it.

After Singapore, I landed in Denver, Colorado, for a quick year. Colorado called to me for its newness, for its nature. And its romance—I had kicked off a long-distance relationship that I felt had a spark worth chasing.

Colorado was my clean slate. I was the new girl in town; I had no family there, no friends, and almost no business connections. At first, there was something sparkly about it all, a chance to recreate myself in an entirely new city. But it quickly grew lonely, and the San Francisco girl inside of me felt out of place. I missed the pulse of San Francisco, the innovation, the hipsters and technologists. I even missed the fog, the pressure, the stacked apartments, and brushing shoulders with strangers on the sidewalk.

It would be a year, but the city would call me back. And when it did, I sprinted for it with the urgency and sure footing of someone who knew she was going home.

NO REGRETS

Failure lurks around every corner. It will find you, no matter how good you are. Failure doesn't care about your long work days or your dedication or your good intent. It's there, always waiting. What a bitch.

My dear personal friend, Tejal Shah, couldn't escape it. Tejal is founder of KidAdmit, a start-up that never completely got its wings. She's one of the most warm and personable people I know. I'm lucky to have been friends with Tejal for many years now, and because of that I've seen her on both sides of the story: while KidAdmit was on the rise and after its doors had to shutter.

The concept behind KidAdmit was making the preschool admissions process seamless for parents, a problem Tejal experienced personally. So many schools, so many requirements, so many forms, so much to read up on—there had to be a better way. Tejal began KidAdmit with gumption, some saved-up personal money, and a bootstrapping mentality. She chose to gain traction before raising capital, skipping the friends and family round (and probably a lot of drama that comes with it!).

Her early strategy was getting as much feedback as possible on her concept and building up her Rolodex of contacts. She was relentless about this—readily asking for advice and gathering thoughts from everyone from VCs to friends to others in the parent-education space. To further round out her concept and come out of the gate strong, she joined Tumml, an urban innovation accelerator with a niche in the space of bettering communities and simplifying lives. Tejal was smart. She knew she needed to solidify her concept and come out strong because, as she said, "You can't just raise money on an idea." You need traction.

Another admirable thing about Tejal: she went into this without trepidation. She dove into the water, headfirst, making it a full-time gig from the start. In other words, she knew what she was getting into. And she had the courage to go into it 100 percent committed. "I know the efforts involved in running a business. You have to put everything into it," she said.

KidAdmit's earliest version served as a directory for parents, but Tejal knew it needed to mature beyond that, a conclusion that was further validated by parents. This meant getting pre-schools on board to help make the sign-up process easier for parents, where KidAdmit would get a revenue cut from the application.

Things were coming together. "I felt like it was the right time to raise money," Tejal said.

She made her pitch deck and researched the heck out of investors, knowing she couldn't just ping anyone. Reaching out to the right person is critical to avoid wasting everyone's time. She knew fundraising was going to be a challenge, but she was met with skepticism from the start. Investors came back to her with lines questioning her commitment (A woman?! Running a start-up with a family and kids?!); she was told she was early—a lot. And that KidAdmit was just not VC-worthy business.

But something happened, despite the initial negativity from investors: KidAdmit grew, from a handful of users to fifty and then a thousand and more. Something was working, her start-up was beginning to stick. Yet she was still told by investors that she was "early," something she found frustrating, something she said was a dual-edged feedback sword. "Most companies don't hit the ground running and have amazing traction right off the bat. It takes trust and blind faith on both ends to invest in that."

One of her earliest lessons, then: cut through the investors and try to get a clear answer earlier on. "Even if you think it's a maybe, it's definitely not a yes. You only want to spend a certain amount of time on those conversations." So, although she sent a ton of follow-up e-mails, she said she wished she had thanked many investors for their time earlier on, with a simple note telling them she'd keep 'em posted. But she admitted that walking away from a potential—however slight—is a tough call. You just don't want to give up.

Tejal learned a lot in her pitching process, including when to send her pitch deck (only if investors explicitly asked for it), how to control a pitch meeting conversation (don't necessarily rely on your deck), and the delicate balance between putting on a performance when sharing your pitch and being confident and casual (tough to do in a giant formal conference room). She admitted that the pitch deck itself can become an obsession. Because she received so much feedback on hers, it was tempting to continuously edit and second-guess everything.

"You can start fixating on your pitch deck," she said. But, ironically, "all the investors who ended up investing, no one looked at the pitch deck . . . so much stress is put into the pitch deck when very little is based on that."

The end of KidAdmit was much like the pilot who runs out of gas midflight. "We didn't close our seed round. We didn't get to what we needed to continue on, and we ran out of money, sadly. I had to wind down the company at the end of 2016," Tejal said.

Just like that, the last part of their seed round didn't come through. It just didn't happen.

Tejal took time to wrap things up and breathe. She said she is extremely proud of her team for how much they accomplished with so few resources. Users and supporters were sad to hear the news.

"I don't think I'll ever get over it," she said. "But I'm okay with that. I'll always be super proud of it, but it didn't work out as intended. It will be something that will stay with me."

The slightly easier part to take: the supporters who told her they loved her but didn't necessarily love the idea. Harder to take: the supporters who ended up doing something in the same space. "That was a bit more hurtful," she reflected. "It absolutely is a grieving process. It's not linear. It's up and down, and you go back and forth through all the stages."

But she's not bitter, and she already knows what she would do differently. "I had great investors. I wish I had some investors who were marketplace operators. Who had done a marketplace start-up. Marketplaces take a long time, you need people who will be in there with you for the long run."

Next time, she will ask more questions. Push harder to get a response. Ask for reasons why they're not interested. Try to get specifics on feedback versus being okay with half answers from investors. Giving feedback to entrepreneurs is something, she said, the industry can improve on.

In the meantime, Tejal has dived right back into the real world. She helped a friend launch a company and swiftly moved on to UrbanSitter, a start-up that focuses on helping parents find childcare, where she does business development work. She obviously loves the industry she's in and is using the expertise she's gained to help UrbanSitter expand.

FAILURE, FAILURE, EVERYWHERE

So, what is it about Silicon Valley and San Francisco that makes us waive our right to failure like it's our freaking slogan?

It's the only place in the world where you can surround yourself with a thick padding of incredibly intelligent, successful people. They are everywhere in this town, absolutely everywhere. Brilliance, opportunity, pure luck—it's out there on every corner. Being around it gives you a sensation of being untouchable. It's like if you get close enough to it, to these people—the ones who have taken on the moonshots and won—that it will rub off on you. That can make it seem like failure's just a quick stop on the way to major success.

But ultimately it's not about the failure. It's about the risk. We exist in a culture of risk taking, one that doesn't exist anywhere else. No other market pushes risk like we do. It's not that we're celebrating the losses—a loss is still a loss, and failing still feels pretty darn crummy—it's that we're celebrating the *risk*. We're high-fiving the leaps, the chances, the maybes, and the what ifs. It's our heartbeat. It's a collective attitude, city-wide, valley-wide: keep on keeping on. And that's something.

That's something I can believe. I buy it.

WHAT DID WE LEARN?

✓ **Failure will find you.**
No one wants to think about it (duh, because it's a drag). But failure will happen. If it doesn't happen in a dramatic start-up shutdown, it will happen in other elements of your life. You won't get that job. You'll screw up that big project. You'll piss off the wrong person. You will partner with the wrong cofounder.

Whatever it is, it's going to come your way. No one sails through start-up life without a few failure pebbles at the bottom of our pockets. Knowing this doesn't make them easier to carry. But it's something to know and to be pragmatic about. You don't need to volunteer for it. And you certainly don't need to celebrate it. But you can work at being more okay with it. (Like, give yourself a break and avoid downing a few bottles of cheap chardonnay if it happens, okay?)

✓ **Despite the failure epidemic, get ready for loneliness.**
It's the secret we all carry but no one wants to talk about. Could you be the one to break this cycle? Maybe. Call a

friend and find out. Talk about it, see what happens. But be okay with how you feel—whether you're raging or sad or feeling flat-out stupid. Try to find a few good eggs to put up with your pints of ice cream and sob stories. And just know that you'll come out on the other side of it in one piece. Tejal and I are examples of that.

✓ It's not about failure, it's about risk.

Change your mind-set. When you fail, just know that you had the guts to go and do something that so few people can do in this world. You just went for it. You took charge of your life. You did the thing that most people are terrified of doing: owning your dreams.

When I put it that way, it almost sounds hip, doesn't it? You stepped off that ledge and made a go of it. Don't be proud that you failed—c'mon, no one is. But be proud that you had the heart and the work ethic and the confidence to go for it. Now, that's something to celebrate.

PART III

On Girls in Tech

CHAPTER 14

What I Know Now

YOU CAN'T GO more than a decade without picking up lessons along the way. I'm grateful to say I've picked up more than a few, even more grateful that I've learned at all, though the journey has felt more like an obstacle course at times, rather than a gentle guiding hand.

These are the teachings that I've learned the hard way—the lessons that have dug deep and left scar tissue. I carry them with me, close to my heart. This isn't a wish to rewrite the past. No, it's nothing that dramatic. It's the stones of wisdom I'll take with me, here at Girls in Tech and wherever I go beyond that.

Some are more practical than others.

Let's start with a less sexy one, shall we? Invest in a good attorney.

If they advertise themselves on a bus bench or run radio commercials that promise to get you out of a Friday night DUI, then they're not for you. If they seem too good to be true— maybe too cheap, too slick, or they're offering to work for free, they're not for you. Walk straight to the nearest exit sign and ask some reputable start-up buddies about who they can refer you to. Remember, your network is always your best bet for a starting line. For pretty much anything.

You need an attorney for all the things you don't know. And you don't know what you don't know. That's a scary thing when you're starting a business, taking checks, shaking hands, and schmoozing with VCs. You're going to go into this whole thing with trepidation. You'll step in slowly, unsure of your every move. But, eventually, you'll gain some confidence, walk a bit straighter, shake hands a little tighter. Just like you're most likely to pull a muscle or get shin splints when you're a beginning runner—you go too far and you're excited and your confidence pushes you beyond the bounds of where your body needs to stop—it can be much the same in Start-up Land. It's just at this moment when you want to take a leap, perhaps a stupid one, or sign some fancy-schmancy legal document—so tempting and crisp on its ivory backdrop—that you need an attorney at your side. The lawyer's goal isn't to block you from the good but to shield you from the bad. Welcome this, run toward it.

It's worth the money. Some things are worth shelling out some dough for, and those things don't all have to do with writing code. I've used attorneys to help define my legal structure. Answer tax-related questions. Guide me in creating board governance guidelines and expectations. Handhold me through intimidating contracts and talk to me like a two-year-old when I need some 'splaining.

I'm not saying you need a worldwide firm or to call in tons of troops. Just get someone reputable with a good head on his or her shoulders who you can trust. They're out there. But, for the love of God, hire a freakin' attorney.

Lesson two: consider an HR consultant.

No one at start-ups hires HR people. No shocker there—typically, you're investing in technologists first and then marketers and sales troops second. Keep going there, don't stop. And, let's face it, HR folks tend to have a funky reputation.

They're the internal police at an organization (now, I *am* cring-ing). The crossing guards, the mall cops. And they're naturally sandwiched between mega loads of conflict: they're being paid by an organization to "help" its employees and enforce policy. Although employees are always told to go to HR when there's a problem, HR is going to side with whoever is cutting their checks. Let's be blunt about it: they're not there for the em-ployees as much as big companies like to say they are. *Say it enough and they'll believe it.* Nope.

That doesn't mean that you won't eventually have to hire an HR person. Full time, baby. But that may not happen un-til you hit fifty, seventy-five, a hundred employees. Make sure you can survive to that scale first. In the meantime, despite my candor, find an HR consultant, someone on the outside that you can lob a few hours to every month. It makes sense for all the reasons I just stated, only, this time, it's in your favor. Get someone on your side who can walk you through grisly policy manuals, employment benefits, nondisclosures, and payroll. The administrative crap and the human stuff. The drama that will naturally bubble up as you grow; that is unavoidable when you get many people from many different backgrounds in the same work space. Now this, this is where HR has an opportunity to shine. *In your favor.*

It's a cover-your-ass type of thing, I'm not going to deny it. Cover. That. Ass. Once you get out of the garage or coworking-space mode, where you have a bit more room to sprawl and suddenly you find yourself second-guessing—do you have eigh-teen employees, or was it twenty-one?—those are signs it's time for an HR consultant.

Maybe this is a good line dance into the next Thing I Know: You can't be friends with your employees. You can be *friendly*. You can grab happy hours. You can listen. You can joke. You can lunch. You can high-five. But you can't really be *friends*. Not in the conventional sense.

I've been burned on this one. A lot. (Okay, borderline-embarrassment a lot.) This has gotten inside my head a bit. It's caused me to think twice about people and their goodness and their intentions. *Look over your shoulder, Adi.* No doubt, this is somewhat related to my issues in hiring too fast. I need to learn to slow down and be deliberate, open my eyes. Friendships included.

What can start out as the chummiest, most bubbly working relationship in the world can quickly sour. It may take time, or it may happen in what feels like a moment, a dispute over a project. Passive-aggressive messages. Battles between team members.

So, now I've learned to keep my distance. I create a little moat between myself and my team. It's not to be cold (far from it!); it's just to protect myself from the drama that may be. This is why I've never understood how founders can partner with their BFFs or husbands to start companies. It seems to work for some, but why take that risk? Why risk losing a relationship that is so wonderful and stable and, well, working, over a business?

So, I'll listen if you have a problem, even if it's not work related. But I won't invite you over on a Friday night to veg with me and wine on my patio. I'll do lunch and happy hour with you every week, but I won't invite you to my birthday party. I'll listen to you rant about your boyfriend, but I won't plan a double date. See the difference?

By the way, this is a two-way street. Start-up employees should strive to avoid being buddy-buddy with their bosses, too. When it comes time to negotiate salary, redline a contract, or jump ship, you don't want those emotional tethers holding you back.

There's a lot of things life is too short for. This is one of them.

Next: hiring slow. Firing faster. As I mentioned before, hiring has been one of my greatest weaknesses as a leader (damn, that's still hard to spit out). I'm constantly backpedaling here, hitting the breaks. *Slow down, think it over before you make an offer.* It's hard to slow down when business operates on an 80 mph highway. There's this constant pressure to get things done, to move faster, to execute. And you need people to do that. When you receive a referral from a friend or even meet someone who seems ambitious at a networking event, there's this impulse to grab your net and swoop that person right up.

But. It's important to not just ask for references but to call them. Dig around and kick up the dust a little. What's that person's story? What does he or she want from you? What are the candidate's strengths and weaknesses? I'm hosing down my own mistakes by hiring as a team. This has been my biggest shield: have your team interview, have your board interview. Get others' perspectives.

I'm working on it, hmmmkay?

What else, what else? Oh, just that little thing called international business. Not one of us operates in a safe little shell. You should kick off your start-up thinking big from day one; you're not the corner bakery, and you can't adopt a mom-and-pop mind-set. In the age of global digitalization, you have to assume you're going to go global because that's where your audience will be, whether it begins that way or not.

Girls in Tech began as a San Francisco gathering of women, but our fourth chapter swiftly popped up in . . . Kuwait. (I was surprised, too.)

Kuwait happened through a friendly connection and a passionate woman who was willing to take on the role of managing director in an area of the world where women fight for their right to choose and to learn and to be individuals every day. It wasn't a part of my plan. The thought never occurred to me that we'd hit the Middle East before we hit markets like Phoenix, Miami, Chicago. I would have thought London or Paris, maybe, but not Kuwait.

But opportunity knocked, serendipitously. And I couldn't say no.

Never make the silly assumption that your business will live on your block and your block alone. If you're thinking that small and you're that shortsighted, then stop what you're doing right now and ask yourself why you're doing it. We're all connected (thank you, internet!). People talk to each other. People travel. They want to take products and technologies with them, wherever they go in the world. What I didn't think about at first was that this meant networks and communities, too.

When you expand into other markets, it's not just about giving it a good luck push and hoping for the best. You have to take cultural considerations and language barriers and societal norms into consideration. Put on your big-girl yoga pants and get flexible—with your product or service, that is. It's helped me that Girls in Tech's managing directors are given the autonomy to orchestrate the programs that will best serve their unique communities. In other words, I'm not dictating, from my throne in San Francisco, what should or shouldn't occur in our chapters in Africa, Australia, or Europe . . . or even San Diego and New York. I'm looking to the managing director to offer insights into what they need and how we can best help.

When you're not physically there, prepare to partner. Big time.

Okay, here's another lesson for you, a big Band-Aid to rip off and choke out: I should have gone full time with Girls in Tech. A long, long time ago. You talk to any serious entrepreneur, and he or she goes full time as soon as possible. Dedicating your all to your start-up is a tenet of entrepreneurship. Talk to any VC with a heartbeat and he'll tell you: why should we take all the risk and write you fat checks and spend our time on your venture when you won't even do it?

Going full time is a display of hardcore dedication and faith and tenacity. It's the best you can do and it's the least you can do, all in one. Moonlighting works for a minute, but it'll fog over your focus and lead to rapid burnout. It's just not sustainable.

I waited to quit until I had my back up against a wall. That's the truth. It wasn't this planned, graceful thing (God, I wish it had been). There wasn't anything seriously strategic about it. I went from job to job and traveled the world and lived my life until an emergency landing was required. Panic set in. My parachute was quitting my day job and hustling to get that initial $95K.

After those terrible first few months, when I got sponsorship support and pulled off the conference (and my hair grew back), I could see more clearly. I should have done it sooner. Girls in Tech would have blossomed faster and gotten organized far sooner had I done so.

I can't pull a Harry Potter and go back in time, but I can think more strategically about my next moves, and that's what I'm digging my heels into, every day.

WHAT DID WE LEARN?

✓ **You're never going to stop learning.**
I don't mean to take a corny spin on this, but it's the truth. You're not perfect, and you won't be in year one or year twenty. This isn't an age thing or an experience thing. You have your entire career in front of you, in and out of the start-up space, to fine-tune your moves. Give yourself the space to do this. Embrace it with humility and gratitude. You have an opportunity, every day, to do something wonderful, to be the best person you can be. Take that and run with it like it's the golden lottery ticket.

✓ **Make your mistakes. And then march forward.**
I can't write this book and pretend I'm perfect. Everyone makes mistakes. Some will eat you up on the inside, and others you'll brush off. The goal is to keep moving forward.

Get your claws out of the past, stop holding on to what's already happened. Your mistakes will serve you best if you keep moving forward and put your stones of wisdom and might-have-beens to use. Today.

✓ Invest in resources, more resources than you would think.

I know it's the thing to be lean and scrappy. To do the ramen thing, to frugal your way to success. But what happened to moderation? There are some resources worth investing in, like an attorney. Don't blow your money mindlessly, but also don't be so cheap and scared to spend that you make an incredibly expensive mistake. Money spent now, in the earliest days of your venture, will come back tenfold in peace of mind and a better, more organized business.

✓ Get over yourself.

You can't learn if your ego is roadblocking the process. Arrogance, ego, selfishness—these will kill your reputation and kill your business. (Remember, no assholes!) Try to be a good human, okay?

CHAPTER 15

What's Next

PEOPLE ALWAYS ASK me if I am going to stick with Girls in Tech, see it through. This question always surprises me, as though I have any other choice. Girls in Tech truly is my baby—a sprawling, international baby. Perhaps it's that way now more than ever. Even though it's been years—more than eleven by now—in many ways, I've come into my own in my "motherhood" of this organization in the past few years alone, because of going full time and making so many changes.

The organization isn't the only thing that's experienced a transformation. I feel like I'm just now reaching my prime. Something has shifted for me, personally and professionally. I've managed to whip up quite a lot of momentum; things feel like they're churning. I have a badass team I can count on. I'm hiring more than ever, and we're at our peak as far as markets and chapter engagement. Sponsors and corporations are seeking us out and asking to brainstorm creative ways to collaborate; it's no longer a one-sided sales pitch. The Catalyst Conference continues to gain traction; we're putting more ambitious women in seats than ever before and getting some truly jaw-dropping business celebs on our stage. In 2017, we took the show on the road to London and Australia to expand our reach to help more women. It's magic, all of it. And it feels good.

It's like being in a spin class and seeing the hills before you on the video monitor and not hesitating for a moment—you're in a zone, and you just keep pumping and going and sweating and breathing right through it. This is a start-up in the growth phase, when you're on the upward climb but you've managed to create enough of a running start to help shove yourself over that hill. And, boy, does being shoved feel good.

Decisions come easier now. I'm in sync with myself, like a grandfather clock that hasn't been tuned in a decade, not even realizing that I doubted myself in the past until now, when I feel so knowing, so assured. *Tick tock*. There's a certain rhythm to my work and my thinking and my days and my weeks. What used to feel at best okay and often downright clumsy is coming easily now.

I've gained confidence I didn't even realize I was missing. Still not perfect, not even close (oh hey, red dress), but better. More fulfilled. I've gained a sense of authority, one that I used to see in others and now I know others see in me because they tell me. When I was in my early twenties, I had no idea that one day I'd receive letters from people telling me that I inspire them, that I motivate them to do more and be better.

To receive letters with words like this, it's both an honor and a call to duty. It raises the bar on my own actions and that of the organization. Yes, we've done a lot, but have we done enough? Yes, we've grown worldwide, but where do we go next?

These questions. These are the things that can keep me up at night.

I know we need to cast a larger reach and nudge our invisible borders beyond that of the United States and areas we've been established in for years now, such as London and Singapore. The world is more volatile, more uncertain than ever. The stakes are higher now. As an organization, we're on track to hit 150 chapters by 2020, specifically targeting devastatingly underserved regions, such as the Middle East and Africa.

Look at it this way. Women in the United States feel trapped every day. The #MeToo movement is a clear portrayal of that. It's 2019 but we're still viewed as objects. We're still treated like toy dolls. We're still so often dismissed, written off, pushed to the outer edge when we should have seats at the center table by now. These stories are real—and the uphill battle before us can't be undermined. This can't be swept under a rug or downplayed.

In other words, we've got work to do.

But take this story—the story of American women—and then crush it. Erase any concept of normalcy. Cross out the resource list and the happy HR programs and the role models and the educational models available to many of us here in the States. Add in a thick layer of violence and oppression, threats, and generations of patriarchal barriers. That's the fight that women in so many far-flung regions face every day.

We have to go there. There is no other way. My work—our work—isn't done until we get there. We're not making progress unless we make progress for all women. We're not taking steps forward if we're leaving so many behind. We can't celebrate— not entirely, not the way we should celebrate—if there are so many women around the globe feeling pain today.

I know when I'll be through with Girls in Tech, when it will be time for me to toss in my hat, lock up the offices, and close up shop for good. I dream of this day. I can see it. I visualize it and step toward it in everything we do. Girls in Tech will be over when there's no need for it to exist. We exist now only because we need to. We're a movement because women need us to be, they need something cohesive to organize and bring all the puzzle pieces together. That's what we're doing.

But can you imagine if women didn't need those pillars? Imagine women on complete parity with men. I'm talking equal pay to men, not having to fight for it like you're a crazy person for wanting to be paid the same for the same work. I'm talking about no more ass grabs at networking events, no more creepy hands brushing by my backside for a moment too long (many moments too long). Imagine opening a textbook in your science class and reading about a revolutionary female scientist, having more women teaching calculus in high school and telling their students about their love of mathematics and numbers and how they power the world; imagine our daughters playing dress-up astronaut and doctor instead of princess, waiting to be saved by a prince. (That's the last thing I want, the thing that makes me stomach-sick. That a woman thinks she needs to be saved by a man, a man in power, a man who thinks he owns her destiny. The Harvey Weinsteins and the Trumps and the Matt Lauers and the Bill Cosbys of the world.)

Imagine more diversity on work teams and in boardrooms and in management ranks, in and outside of Silicon Valley. Think about how this could alter the lives of women: they might feel like they could have a child and still thrive at work because they no longer are forced to choose. There's a sense of equilibrium at home and in the workplace, a sense of partnership and a balancing of the scales. This is where real innovation can occur—mind-blowing innovation—when you get so many people in a room, and they all have different lenses and personal beliefs and problems and colors and wins. To come at a problem from so many angles has the potential to be groundbreaking in a way that no technology today can. This level of collaboration and diversity can't be mimicked by artificial intelligence, and certainly not by a room full of white tech guys in hoodies.

To those of you who think things are rolling along just fine, I say, screw the status quo. Give me an argument that will convince me that we're fine. These problems are not okay. The day we accept them is the day we give up. The day they are gone is the day Girls in Tech becomes more of a network than a movement. That is the day I'm fighting for.

So, we'll continue to expand around the world. I'll continue to build out my team. We're adding more structure and support than ever for our chapters, including more tools at their disposal like event ticketing, custom websites, and fundraising support. We've learned a few lessons in the ways of partnerships and sponsorships—and the result is deeper partnerships and more engaged connections, more value, more influence. Something is working; we've found our stride.

And a few new initiatives I'm thrilled about: we're on the cusp of opening our own, in-house coding school, CODE GIT. This means hands-on, in-person training for women of all ages to help them prepare for the real world and master the skills they need to survive and thrive in tech. Right now, we're tweaking our curriculum, hiring instructors, and finishing the core components of the program build. Additionally, we're launching our own recruitment platform, a job site that exclusively focuses on our vast community of women in STEM. This will be a tool for progressive companies to gain access to our community and expose their brand to these amazing women. And it will be a place for women to get career advice, find the job they've been searching for—and go for it knowing that they're among a community of friends.

We are creating a completely integrated suite of programs, proven programs, that can change the forecast for women around the world. We're arming them with knowledge. We're empowering them with confidence. We're enabling them to live the lives they've dreamed of.

This is why Girls in Tech is here, and this is why we're growing.

And this is why I'm not going anywhere.

ACKNOWLEDGMENTS AND GRATITUDE

I'VE ALWAYS WANTED to create a book to share my journey through life and Silicon Valley. It's been a wild ride, one I've always had the desire to share, not just to knock off a bucket list item but to connect with my audience and peers on a deeper level. My goal with this book was to pull the curtain on Silicon Valley: to expose the circus behind the scenes, the ironies, the hardships and then get real about what it takes to survive it. So, thank you, readers, for listening.

Thank you to my mother and father. You have been there for me throughout every stage of my career, not just as the parents that you are but as my best friends, through and through. You're always in my corner, always there to listen, and your support is tenacious, unwavering, and true. I know how lucky I am to have you.

Thank you to Joanna Furlong, my coauthor on this project. Without your dedication and collaboration, this book would not have been possible.

I also want to thank all the Tech Boss Ladies in my life. How fortunate I am to be surrounded by such an extraordinary network of women! Ladies, you power my every day. Thank you for your sisterhood and for being a network I can turn to, time and time again, for advice and strength.

Thank you to the elite group of intelligent and inspirational women who were kind enough to open their hearts, minds, and histories to us for this book, our interviewees. Thank you for being so willing to share your stories and advice and for being so generous with your time.

Thanks to my powerhouse book team! To Anthony Mattero, for being an agent extraordinaire, and to the smooth team at Foundry Media. Also, thank you to Stephanie Knapp, my stellar editor at Seal Press, for her patience and expertise. Thank you both for believing in this idea and for believing in me.

Thank you to Girls in Tech's board of directors. We've come a long way together, and together we've achieved incredible things. I'm looking forward to growing the organization with you and to continuing to partner together to change the world.

To my Girls in Tech corporate staff and extensive team of consultants: you rock! Thank you for showing up, for dealing with the crazy days, for being creative geniuses, and for always pulling through, every time.

Thank you to the international network of Girls in Tech managing directors and their advisory boards. You are the true heroes of this organization. Without your commitment, long hours, and huge hearts, I simply couldn't do it.

Thank you to the thousands of friends and supporters of Girls in Tech. I'm continually amazed at the support we have around the world, at the people like you who are so kind and so willing to give (and then give more, and then give again). Don't ever underestimate my appreciation.

And, finally, I want to thank Silicon Valley and San Francisco for being such a dynamic backdrop for this book and for real life. Your energy, your pulse, your quirks and innovation light up the hearts and minds—and ignite the brilliance—of people all around the world. And I get to walk your streets every day and be a part of your community and get carried along in the current of your inventiveness. Now, that's nothing short of amazing.

NOTES

CHAPTER 1

1. Mackay, Harvey. (2017, Nov. 15). Harvey Mackay: The Importance of Being Urgent. Daily Herald. Retrieved from: http://www.heraldextra.com/business/harvey-mackay-the-importance-of-being-urgent/article_2ea92d65-ceed-5121-a350-6ebb54d180fa.html
2. Suster, Mark. (2010, Jan. 5). What Makes an Entrepreneur? Cojones (7/11). Both Sides of the Table. Retrieved from: https://bothsidesofthetable.com/what-makes-an-entrepreneur-cojones-7-11-bd05cb0ab9f2

CHAPTER 2

1. Valentina, Zarya. (2018, Jan. 31). Female Founders Got 2% of Venture Capital Dollars in 2017. Fortune. Retrieved from: http://fortune.com/2018/01/31/female-founders-venture-capital-2017/

CHAPTER 3

1. Mytton, David. (2017, May 13). Can Google's 20% Time Really Work for Your Startup? VentureBeat. Retrieved from: https://venturebeat.com/2017/05/13/can-googles-20-time-really-work-for-your-startup/

CHAPTER 5

1. Panic Attack Diagnosis. Silicon Valley. YouTube video, posted by Thrift Fowl, April 7, 2014. Retrieved from https://www.youtube.com /watch?v=l8qB0DOZ9MY

CHAPTER 6

1. Suster, Mark. (2011, May 9). The Co-founder Mythology. Both Sides of the Table. Retrieved from: https://bothsidesofthetable.com/the -co-founder-mythology-7919a32e17c8

CHAPTER 10

1. Furlong, Joanna. Key Takeaways from the Girls in Tech Catalyst Conference, Part I. Retrieved from http://girlsintech.org/2016/04/key -takeaways-from-the-girls-in-tech-catalyst-conference-part-i/

CHAPTER 11

1. Scorpio, Jessica. (2012, May 12). How to Win Disrupt, Tips from Getaround. TechCrunch. Retrieved from: https://techcrunch .com/2012/05/15/how-to-win-disrupt-tips-from-getaround

INDEX

Abrams, Jonathan, xxiii
AdSense, 37
advice to entrepreneurs
    admit mistakes and move on,
        195–196
    be willing to go full time with
        start-up, 194–195
    get over your ego, 196
    hire an HR consultant,
        190–191
    invest in good attorney,
        189–190
    invest in resources, 196
    keep learning, 195
    maintain professional distance
        from employees, 191–192
    pay attention to international
        business possibilities,
        193–194
advisors, 81–97
    board of directors, 86–92
    building connections, 92–94
    circle of trust, 95, 97
    formal role in start-up
        environment, 84, 86

Fran Maier's experience as,
    84–85
role played by, 81–83
advisory team, 84
Airbnb, 50, 84, 117, 119, 125,
    127
Akamai, 110
Amazon, 69
Amazon Web Services, 92
AMPLIFY pitch competition,
    148–150
AngelList, 176
Antar, Alvina, 105–109
apps, to find cofounders, 74
asking for help
    about stress, 65–66
    from board of directors,
        90, 96
    business for good and, 46, 52
    women and, 28
asshole, leadership and not being
    an, 169–171, 173–174
Athena Alliance, 87
attention to detail, entrepreneurs
    and, 13

attorney
    investing in good, 189–190
    need for in negotiations with
        venture capital, 159

Basecamp, 12–13
benefits of intrapreneurship, 40
Bezos, Jeff, 69
Bird, Sarah, 138–141
Blank, Steve, 120
Blockbuster, 118
board of directors, 86–92
    asking for help from, 90, 96
    diversity issue, 87
    managing, 86, 88–92, 96
    as peers, 96
    what company receives in
        exchange for board seat, 88
body language, conveying
    confidence, 135
boundaries, stress and setting, 64,
    65
Boyer, Donna, 125, 126–128
brand value, understanding own,
    112
Brown, Coco, 87, 88, 89, 90
bullies, confronting, 170–171
burnout, 60–62
business for good, 43–52
    SheEO and, 43–48
    start-ups, values, and, 48–51
business school networks,
    93–94

career recruitment platform, 14
Carter, Sandy, 92
Catalyst Conference, 172
    expansion of, 197–198
    first, 14–16, 62, 63
    "O Conference" and, 31

presenters at, 44, 143
    See also Girls in Tech
change, founders and acceptance
    of, 120–121
charity, linking up with, 49
Chase Communications, xvii
children, familiarity with
    technology, 118–119
CIO (chief information officer),
    hiring, 106–107
circle of trust, advice from, 95,
    97
CODE GIT coding school, Girls
    in Tech, 201
cofounders, 10, 67–70, 71–72
    apps to help find, 74
    Cara Delzer's experience with,
        72–74
    confidence and, 71–72
    evaluating, 74, 75–76, 78–79
    polarizing issue of, 67–68
    sole founder vs., 69, 70–71
    split among, 76, 78
    when relationship does not
        work, 74–76
CoFoundersLab, 74
community value, of start-ups,
    48–51
competitors, knowing services or
    products of, 121
confidence, 131–145
    author's lack of preparation
        and, 142–143
    author's sense of own, 133–135,
        198
    body language and, 135
    cofounders and, 71–72
    earned, 143–144
    entrepreneurs and, 9, 131–133,
        138

making major life changes and,
    135–136
the pitch and, 150
preparation and, 140–143, 145
reframing stories and, 137, 144
risk aversion and, 137
Sarah Bird's story of coping
    with own, 138–141
confidence gap, women and, 139
corporate jobs, experience of
    working in, xvii
creativity
    creating company that fosters,
        123–124
    intrapreneurship and, 32–33, 41
Crew, Amanda, 57
cross-functional development,
    109
Crossroads Coach, 136–137
crowdfunding, testing product
    via, 122
Cuddy, Amy, 135
culture of respect, embedding,
    170
customers
    co-innovation with early,
        122–125, 129
    product-market fit and, 123
    response to innovation, 120

data
    hiring data and analytics
        manager, 107
    innovation and, 130
    pitch deck and, 156
    product development and, 126,
        129–130
decision-making authority
    being clear on who has, 76
    sole founders and, 70–71

decisions
    ease of making, 198
    empowering employees to
        make, 108
    values and business, 43
    values informing business, 49
De Luca, Mercedes, 12–13
Delzer, Cara, 72–74
DFJ, 154
Disclosing New Worlds (Spinosa),
    44–45
discomfort, intrapreneurship and,
    39–40, 41
diversity
    on board of directors, 87
    lack of, in venture capital, 158
    lack of in tech, 27
    leadership and cultural,
        168–169
    in Silicon Valley, 200
dressing for confidence,
    134–135
Dweck, Carol, 11

ego
    getting over one's own, 196
    in venture capital, 152
embarrassment of failure, 176
employees, as work friends, 102,
    191–192
entrepreneurs
    advice to (see lessons learned)
    allowing intrapreneurship, 40
    among author's family, xv,
        xvi–xvii, 3–7
    author's experience in
        becoming, 14–16
    confidence and, 131–133, 138
    De Luca on what it takes,
        12–13

entrepreneurs (*continued*)
    focus and, 17
    growth mind-set of, 11, 17
    as job creators, 5
    lack of fear among, 3, 7–10, 16
    risk and, 13
    Roizen on what it takes, 10–12
    sense of urgency and, 8, 17
    stress and, 57–60
    Suster on traits of, 13–14
    what sets entrepreneurs apart,
        3–4, 7–10
    willingness to go full time,
        194–195
    See also founders
entrepreneurship
    author's first experience with,
        xv, xvi–xvii
    defined, 44–45
e-Vangel, 74–75
Eventbrite, 34–36
eye contact, projecting confidence
    and, 135

Facebook, xxiii, 25, 119
failure, 175–186
    author's experience with, 175,
        177–181
    characteristics of, 176–177
    intrapreneurship and
        organizational support for,
        36–37
    loneliness of, 185–186
    Silicon Valley culture and,
        184–185
    taking risks and, 186
    Tejal Shah's experience with,
        181–184
Falzone, Lisa, 60–62
family investment offices, 153

fear
    of asking, 46–47
    entrepreneurs' lack of, 3, 7–10,
        16
feedback
    from advisors, 93
    hiring and medium for, 104
financial situation, investigating
    possible cofounder's, 75, 78
firing employees who do not
    work out, 192–193
focus, entrepreneurs' need for,
    11–13, 17
Fortune (magazine), 22
FounderDating, 74
founders
    allowing employees to make
        own decisions, 108–109
    innovation and, 120–122,
        128
    need to deliver the pitch,
        147–148, 149–150,
        160–163
    possible dwindling control of,
        87
    preparing for board meetings,
        89–90
    relation to board of director,
        87, 88–89
    starting the day with your
        team and setting the tone,
        167–168, 173
    women as, 20, 22
    See also entrepreneurs;
        partners; sole founders
freelance workers, hiring,
    104–105
friends, work *vs.* "real-world," 102,
    191–192
Friendster, xxiii

fundraising
  for Girls in Tech, 15–16, 38,
    62, 91, 201
  See also the pitch; venture
    capital

Garrity, Steve, 70
gender, confidence gap and, 139
Getaround, 76, 156–157,
  159–160
Girls in Tech
  AMPLIFY pitch competition,
    148–150
  author moving from part-time
    to full-time at, 14–16, 62,
    194–195
  author's continuing role in,
    197–199, 201
  board of directors, 90–92
  CODE GIT coding school, 201
  continued expansion of,
    198–199, 201
  early focus on networking
    events and panel discussions,
    xxiv–xxv
  embedding culture of respect
    in, 170
  expansion of, xxiv, xxv
  first event, xxiii–xxiv
  future of, 199–201
  "girls" in name of, xxi–xxiii
  hiring for, 99–102, 103–104
  International Women's Day
    campaign, 29–30
  intrapreneurship at, 29–30,
    37–39
  membership, xxvi
  networking events, xxiii–xxiv,
    xxiv–xxv
  pitching, 160–161
  start of, xix–xxi
  technology as enabler of, 48–49
  trademarked programs, xxv
  See also Catalyst Conference
Girls in Tech Kuwait, xxiv, xxv,
  193
Glitch (game), 32–33
Gmail, 37
Golden Seeds, 167
Goldstein, Talia, 23–25
Google, 25
  project experimentation at, 37
growth, intrapreneurship and, 36
growth mind-set of entrepreneur,
  11, 17

harassment, of women at male-
    dominated start-ups, xviii–
    xix, 19–20, 26–27
Hartz, Julia, 34, 35, 39
Hearsay Social, 70
herd mentality, in venture capital,
  152–153
Herrin, Jessica, 93–94
hiring, 99–116
  advice from Alvina Antar,
    105–109
  advice from Alyson Welch,
    109–112
  author's experience with, 99–
    102, 103–104
  CIO, 106–107
  as companies scale up, 105–106
  culture of respect and, 170
  freelance workers, 104–105
  HR consultant, 190–191
  for leadership, 108–109, 115
  people problems, 112–114
  preparation for, 115
  product managers, 125–127

hiring (*continued*)
 questions to ask about reasons
  for hire, 103–104
 recruitment, 100
 sales team, 109–112
 significance of, 102–103
 slowing pace of, 192–193
hours a week required for
 particular job, 103
human resources consultant,
 hiring, 190–191

idea, innovation and, 120, 121
ideation, creating company that
 fosters, 123–124
innovation, 117–130
 co-innovation with early
  customers, 122–125, 129
 concept of, 117–119
 data and, 130
 encouraging, 119–122
 founders setting culture for,
  128–129
 intrapreneurship and, 32–33,
  41
 organizational culture and, 109
 product development and,
  125–128, 129–130
 starts on the inside, 128–129
Intel Insider program, 31–32
international business
 possibilities, paying attention
 to, 193–194
International Women's Day,
 29–30
intrapreneurship, 29–41
 author and, 30–32
 benefits of, 40
 creativity and, 41
 demand for, 33–39

discomfort and, 39–40, 41
entrepreneurs allowing, 40
failure and, 36–37
at Girls in Tech, 29–30, 37–39
innovation and, 32–33, 41
organizational culture
 supporting, 34–36

job creation, entrepreneurs and,
 5
job posting, 100, 101
journal, employee, 38–39

KidAdmit, failure of, 181–184
knowledge, confidence and, 141,
 145
Kumra, Raina, 151–154
Kuwait, Girls in Tech in, xxiv,
 xxv, 193

"Lady Brags," 30, 38
leadership, 165–174
 advice from veteran leader,
  167–169
 assholes, 169–171, 173–174
 cultural diversity and, 168–169
 doing the right thing for team
  members, 171–173, 174
 hiring for, 108–109, 115
 listening and, 169, 172, 173
 managing stress and, 168
 setting tone for the day,
  167–168, 173
 start-up, 165–167
 women in tech and women in,
  20, 22
leap of faith, entrepreneurs', 13
learning, entrepreneurship and,
 195
lessons learned, 189–196

admit mistakes and move on, 195–196
be willing to go full time with start-up, 194–195
get over your ego, 196
hire an HR consultant, 190–191
invest in good attorney, 189–190
invest in resources, 196
keep learning, 195
maintain professional distance from employees, 191–192
pay attention to international business possibilities, 193–194
LinkedIn, 85, 91, 176
listening, leadership and, 169, 172, 173
loneliness, of failure, 185–186

Mackay, Harvey, 8
Maier, Fran, 84–85
M&A (mergers and acquisitions), 23
managing
board of directors, 86, 88–92, 96
people problems, 112–114
stress, 168
market, warming up the, 111–112
Match.com, 74, 84
Mavin, 151–154
meetings
board, 89–90
scrum, 121
showing up for, 114
membership, Girls in Tech, xxvi

men, role in lifting women up in tech, 20–21
#MeToo movement, 19, 25, 199
millennials, working for companies with values aligned to their own, 48
Mindset: The New Psychology of Success (Dweck), 11
mind-set of entrepreneur, 11, 17
mistakes, moving on from, 195–196
Mockus, Darrell, 74–75
Moxxly, 72–74
Moz, 138–141
MVP (minimum viable product), 120, 121, 123

negotiating, venture capital funding, 159
Netflix, 118
network, building, 92–94, 97
networking events, Girls in Tech, xxiii–xxiv, xxiv–xxv
The No Asshole Rule: Building a Civilized Workplace and Surviving One That Isn't (Sutton), 170

"O Conference," 31
Ogilvy & Mather, 31–32
online video start-up, author's experience in, xviii–xix, 11–12
Opportu Startup Innovation, 119
organizational culture
innovation and, 109, 128–129
supporting intrapreneurship, 34–36
values and, 43
organizational retreats, 172

Panafold, 167
panel discussions, Girls in Tech, xxiv
parenting, child's focus and, 13
partners, 67–79
  apps to help find, 74
  Cara Delzer's experience with, 72–74
  to close the gaps, 77–78
  cofounders, 67–70, 71–72
  evaluating, 74, 75–76, 78–79
  sole founder *vs.*, 69, 70–71
  that are not cofounders, 77
  that are not given 50-50 split, 76, 78
  when cofounder relationship fails, 74–76
personal situation, investigating possible cofounder's, 75, 78
personal sting of failure, 176–177
physical location of job, 103
the pitch, 147–163
  generic pitch template, 154–155
  overview, 147–150
  pitch deck, 153–156, 162, 182, 183
  presentation of, 156–160, 163
  reality of, 161–162
  setting aside time to work on pitching each week, 162
  TechCrunch Disrupts and, 147
  venture capital and, 150–161
PitchBook, 23
pitch deck, 153–156, 162
  Tejal Shah's, 182, 183
planning process, entrepreneurs and, 8–9, 10
power colors, confidence and, 134–135

power poses, 135
practicing pitch, 159–160, 163
pregnancy, women founder seeking venture capital during, 23–25
preparation
  confidence and, 140–143, 145
  of pitch, 159–160, 163
presentation of the pitch, 156–160, 163
pricing, mapping out, 112
private equity, 23
procrastination, 9–10
product development, 125–128
  early customers and, 124–125
  priorities and, 128
  prototypes and, 127
  testing and, 127
  testing via crowdfunding, 122
productivity, entrepreneurs and need for, 12–13
product managers, 125–127
product-market fit, customers and, 123
project-management system, 10
prototypes, 127
public relations team, presenting pitch and, 160

"real-world" friends, 102, 191–192
recruitment, 100
references, checking, 193
reframing stories, confidence and, 137, 144
remote workers, hiring, 104
resiliency, entrepreneurs and, 8
resources
  of board members, 88
  investing in, 196

retreats, organizational, 172
Revel Systems POS, 60–61
RewardsPay, 76
risk
    entrepreneurs and willingness
        to accept, 13
    failure and taking, 185, 186
    venture capital and appetite
        for, 152
risk aversion, confidence and, 137
RocketSpace, 29
Roizen, Heidi, 10–12, 154–155
Rosenberg, Marnie, 135–137
RxMatch, 14

SaaS company, 123
sales, hiring team, 109–112
San Francisco
    acceptance of right to fail in,
        184–185
    author's career path and,
        xvii–xviii, 94, 180
Saunders, Vicki, 43–48
Scorpio, Jessica, 76, 156–157,
        158–159
Screenhero, 123
scrum meetings, 121
sexual harassment, of women in
        tech, xviii–xix, 19–20,
        26–27
Shah, Tejal, 181–184
shame, failure and, 176
SheEO, 43–44, 46–47
Shih, Clara, 70
Shukla, Anu, 76
Silicon Valley
    acceptance of right to fail in,
        184–185
    venture capital networks in,
        158–159

Silicon Valley (television series),
        57–58
skills gaps, hiring to fill, 103
Slack, 32–33
Slide (club), xxiii, xxiv
Snap, 123
sole founders, 69, 70–71
    advantages of being, 70–71
    disadvantages of being, 71
Spinosa, Charles, 44–45
split, between cofounders, 76, 78
Stanford University, 10
start-up leadership. See leadership
start-ups
    author's experience working in
        online video, xviii–xix, 11–12
    community value and, 48–51
    experience of working in, xvii
    loans to female-led, 43–44,
        46–47
    stereotypes of, xviii
    stress and, 57–60, 63
    values, doing the right thing,
        and, 48–51
Stella and Dot, 93
STEM, women and girls and,
        21–22, 25–26, 201
stereotypes, start-up, xviii
Stitch Fix, 125
strategic discussions with board,
        89
stress, 55–66
    author's experience with,
        55–57, 59–60, 62–65
    burnout, 60–62
    compartmentalizing, 60
    confiding about, 65–66
    leadership and managing, 168
    setting boundaries to combat,
        64, 65

stress (*continued*)
  start-ups and, 57–60, 63
  surviving, 62–65
  underestimating, 65
Suster, Mark, 13–14, 70
Sutton, Robert, 170

talent bench, cultivating, 115
talent pipeline, lack of women in,
    20–21
team-building, 99–100. *See also*
    hiring
team management
  people problems, 112–114
  time for, 116
team members
  leadership and showing
    appreciation for, 171–173,
    174
  start-up, 69, 77–78
TechCrunch Disrupts, 147
  Getaround's pitch at, 157,
    159–160
tech industry, hostility towards
    women in, xx. *See also* sexual
    harassment
technology, children's comfort
    level with, 118–119
TED talk on confidence, 135
template, generic pitch, 154–155
tenacity, entrepreneurs and, 11
term sheets, 158
testing, product development
    and, 127, 155, 157
thinking outside the box, 51
Three Day Rule, 23–25
time
  given by board members, 88
  for team management, 116
  to work on pitching, 162

Tiny Speck, 32–33
top metrics, board review of, 89
Trello, 123
trust, hiring and, 101
trusting your gut
  hiring and, 103
  leadership and, 171
20 percent rule, 37

Uber, 20, 118, 119
UrbanSitter, 184
urgency, entrepreneurs' sense of,
    8, 17

values
  business decisions and, 43
  cofounders and shared, 74
  start-ups, business for good,
    and, 48–51
venting, leadership and listening
    to, 169
venture capital, 150–161
  appetite for risk and, 152
  ego and, 152
  failure at obtaining, 182–183
  herd mentality and, 152–153
  lack of diversity in, 158
  negotiating with, 159
  pitching to, 151–154
  start-ups eligible for, 150–151
  term sheets and, 158
  tight networks of Silicon Valley,
    158–159
  women vying for, 22–25
virality, jumpstarting chain of
    customers via, 123
vision, entrepreneurial, 8

warming up the market, 111–112
Weber, Hilary, 119–122, 123, 124

Welch, Alyson, 109–112
Wells, Alice, 142
Winfrey, Oprah, 31
Withgott, Meg, 167–169
Women 2.0 conference, 84
women in tech, 19–28
  asking for help, 28
  confidence gap and, 139
  as founders, 20, 22
  hostility of tech industry
    towards, xx
  lack of women in talent
    pipeline, 20–21
  need to support each other, 27,
    28
  reality for, 19–20

role for men in lifting women
  up, 20–21
sexual harassment of, xviii–xix,
  19–20, 26–27
STEM and, 21–22, 25–26, 201
in upper management, 20, 22
venture capital and, 22–25
women, babies, and start-ups,
  23–25
work friends, 102, 191–192
work styles, hiring and, 104

Zenefits, 20
Zoom video, 123
Zuckerberg, Mark, 167
Zuora, 105, 107–108